GLORY DAYS

Cunard

CARONIA

PLYMOUTH PRESS

Ian Allan
PUBLISHING

David L. Williams

Front cover:
The *Queen Mary* in the Solent, off Gilkicker Point, Hampshire, inward bound to Southampton. *Barry Elliot*

Back cover:
The *Mauretania* (II) in the River Mersey assisted by tugs of the Alexandra Towing Co.
Tom Rayner Collection

Title page:
The *Caronia* during a call at Cape Town. *Ian Shiffmann*

CONTENTS

Acknowledgements	2
Bibliography	2
Introduction	3
1. The Atlantic Express Service after World War 1	5
2. Intermediates and the Dominion Trade	14
3. Amalgamation and the Two-Ship Express Service	23
4. Cruising in the Depression Years	33
5. Auxiliary Service in the War at Sea	41
6. Resumption of the Atlantic Ferry	50
7. The Dominion Services – the Final Decades	63
8. Serious Cruising	70
9. Glory in Transition	82
Fleet List of Principal Passenger Ships 1920-70	93

First published 1998

ISBN 0 7110 2607 6 (Ian Allan Publishing)
ISBN 1-882663-40-3 (Plymouth Press)

Published by Ian Allan Publishing

an imprint of Ian Allan Publishing Ltd, Terminal House, Station Approach, Shepperton, Surrey TW17 8AS.
Printed by Ian Allan Printing Ltd, Riverdene Business Park, Molesey Road, Hersham, Surrey KT12 4RG.

Code: 9811/B2

Acknowledgements

I would like to record my appreciation for the assistance received from the following persons and organisations, without which this book could not have been realised: Associated Press (Joan Fisher), Michael Cassar, Cunard Steamship Company (Eric Flounders), Alex Duncan, Imperial War Museum, Richard de Kerbrech, Lloyd's Shipping Information Services (Norman Hooke), Maritime Photo Library (Adrian Vicary), the late Tom Rayner, *Southern Daily Echo*, Table Bay Underway Shipping, University of Glasgow, Business Archives & Records Centre, University of Liverpool – Cunard Archives, World Ship Photo Library. I am particularly grateful to Philip Rentell and Ian Shiffmann whose help, respectively, with original printed postcards and with photographs really made the colour sections of this book possible.

Bibliography

Bathe, Basil, *Seven Centuries of Sea Travel*, Barrie & Jenkins
Braynard, Frank O., *Lives of the Liners*, Cornell Maritime Press
de Kerbrech, Richard P. and Williams, David L., *Damned by Destiny*, Teredo Books
de Kerbrech, Richard P. and Williams, David L., *Cunard White Star Liners of the 1930s*, Conway Maritime Press
Haws Duncan, *Merchant Fleets in Profile*, Vol 2, Patrick Stephens
Kludas, Arnold, *Great Passenger Ships of the World*, Vols 1-5, Patrick Stephens
Le Fleming, H. M., *Cunard White Star Liners of the 1930s*, Ian Allan
Maxtone-Graham, John, *Tribute to a Queen*, Berlitz Publications
Newell, Gordon, *Ocean Liners of the 20th Century*, Superior Publishing
Rentell, Philip, *Historic Cunard Liners*, Atlantic Transport Publishers
Rentell, Philip, *Historic White Star Liners*, Blue Water Publications
Wall, Robert, *Ocean Liners*, Collins
Williams, David L., *Liners in Battle Dress*, Conway Maritime Press
Williams, David L., *Wartime Disasters at Sea*, Patrick Stephens
Wilson, R. M., *The Big Ships*, Cassell

INTRODUCTION

The ocean passenger ship is, without any question of doubt, the greatest of all man-made constructions, especially as exhibited at its peak of development, from the 1930s onwards. They were as large then as any skyscraper or any of the world's greatest railway stations. But unlike those edifices, locked to the earth, static upon their foundations, ocean passenger ships, fitted with machinery as large as that of a power station, were powerful, mobile monuments of man's engineering prowess. Cleaving the waves at anything up to 30kt, they were truly floating cities.

Of course, other, equally large, ocean vessels have been built – large crude oil tankers and aircraft carriers to name just two. Yet none of these has incorporated the same level of complexity or ornamentation as that which is characteristic of the ocean liner. Passengers, as their 'cargo', required creature comforts, as far as possible 'a real home from home' which could delude them into feeling far removed from the ocean's fury (only a hull's thickness away), as if they were still on dry land.

Thus, there was great competition to provide the most luxurious and most extravagant fittings aboard ship possible. The result was magnificent, lavishly decorated cabins and public rooms of a standard that more than favourably compared with the grandest of hotels or stateliest of mansions.

Great Britain was right at the forefront of the introduction and development of the ocean passenger ship and remained the leading force in scheduled passenger ship operation throughout its long era from the early 1840s to the beginning of the 1970s. Over those 130-odd years various companies came and went as they experienced mixed fortunes in this trade which, more than any other, demanded brave investors, innovative engineers and a truly entrepreneurial spirit in order to succeed.

Some famous names arose to dominate the passenger trade and none more so than two British companies, which today are still household names yet which hold the distinction of having been there at the outset. They were among the earliest pioneers of steam propulsion at sea and are still trading in the ocean passenger business today, albeit now only operating cruises. They are namely the Cunard Steamship Company, founded by Samuel Cunard and partners in 1840 and the Peninsular & Oriental Steam Navigation Company, established in 1837 by Brodie McGhie Willcox and Arthur Anderson. In truth, neither Cunard nor P&O were known originally by their present names but in both cases they are the same company that was launched all those years ago.

Between them, Cunard and P&O have operated no fewer than 700 or so ships (the former 250 and the latter 450), probably a record in itself. Cunard served and dominated the North Atlantic service to the United States and Canada; P&O maintained a complex schedule of routes to India, the Far East and Australasia and was the first choice for the majority of passengers travelling to that part of the globe. Both companies were market leaders in their respective sectors and both set the standard to beat in terms of quality of service, reliability, comfort and safety. It is likely, too, that they were among the very few shipping companies that ever operated profitably, a matter which has, no doubt, largely accounted for their long survival.

From its small origins, early in the 19th century, ocean steamship travel grew steadily. Each year there were more new ships and more and more passengers to fill them. The growth seemed as if it would never end. The peak was reached over a 50-year period which began around 1920, when engineering advances and changed social expectations generated an unprecedented level of demand for ocean travel among all classes of passenger. At that time the youthful air transportation industry presented no challenge whatsoever, so, with shipyards capable of producing larger, faster and more spacious ships than ever before, an era of unrivalled ocean passenger travel was set

to unfold. For Cunard and P&O these were indeed the 'Glory Days'!

Cunard and P&O were, of course, well established companies by 1920 but they had not yet achieved the status of glory which was ultimately to become associated with them. In this regard the next 50 years were to be significant. 'Glory' certainly implies, if it does not actually mean, such things as excellence, splendour, superiority and renown, all of them accolades which by 1970 were richly deserved by Cunard and P&O, having carried all before them on the ocean highways.

Back in 1920, the Cunard Line was recovering from World War 1. The company's ships had served the nation extremely well during the four years of fighting but it had cost it dear. In total it had lost 10 vessels from its passenger fleet, most conspicuously the express turbine steamship *Lusitania* in 1915, sister to the Blue Riband holder *Mauretania* and a former record breaker herself. The other losses were the *Franconia* and *Alaunia* in 1916, the *Ivernia*, *Laconia* and *Ultonia* in 1917 and the *Andania*, *Aurania*, *Ausonia* and *Carpathia* in 1918. For Cunard, the war had got progressively worse. Now these ships had to be replaced if Cunard was to recover its elevated ranking in the ocean passenger business. In the years that followed Cunard did just that, introducing no fewer than 13 new passenger vessels over the period to 1925, many of them reviving the names of those ships which had been the victims of the war at sea. Simultaneously, it took the surviving express ships in hand, overhauled them and converted them to oil fuel, giving them a new lease of life.

All in all, these efforts contributed to the rapid restoration of Cunard's prestige, confirming the company's leading position as it entered its most glorious half century of operation.

Great companies, like all highly regarded institutions, owe their superiority to great leadership and Cunard was no exception to this rule. An important milestone in the affairs of the Cunard Line occurred in 1919 which was to have a profound effect on the company's fortunes over the next half century, successively placing at the helm a sequence of influential, perceptive chairmen who would

direct it through its most glorious era. In 1911 the long-established Liverpool shipping company of Edward Bates & Sons acquired half the shares in the Brocklebank Line of cargo shippers. Eight years later, when Brocklebank and Cunard amalgamated, the Bates brothers (Edward's sons) emerged as a powerful driving force whose executive policies were fundamental to the elevation of the company to the status of renown it enjoyed over the 50 years from 1920.

Sir Percy E. Bates, who had first joined the Cunard board in a non-executive capacity in 1912, was appointed Chairman in 1930, personally driving the 'Big Ship' policy which resulted in the first two great 'Queen' liners. His successor as Chairman, in 1946, was Frederick A. Bates. He was to be the prime mover in once more restoring the battered fleet to its pre-eminent position following the ravages of World War 2. Finally, in 1953, the third brother, Col Denis Bates took over at the top, negotiating the Line through the difficult period of the late 1950s when aircraft competition first began to bite. To him fell the responsibility of perpetuating the 'Big Ship' policy such that, though ultimately modified to reflect the changing expectations of the passenger shipping market, the *Queen Elizabeth 2* was turned from dream into reality.

Between them, these three gentlemen, largely unsung personalities, contributed as much to the achievement of Cunard's celebrated status as ever did their illustrious forbear, the Line's founder, Samuel Cunard.

This book, one of a pair (readers may also be interested in the companion title *Glory Days: P&O*), deals with a timeless, even – as far as the shipping buff is concerned – familiar story. Much has been written on the subject of Cunard previously so it contains few surprises, but that is not its purpose. Rather, it is a celebration in words and pictures of one of Great Britain's greatest passenger shipping companies in the period in which it was at the peak of its ascendancy.

David L. Williams
Newport, Isle of Wight
June 1998

1. THE ATLANTIC EXPRESS SERVICE AFTER WORLD WAR 1

The Cunard Line had briefly established a three-ship express transatlantic service in the summer of 1914, permitting a regular sailing from either side of the Atlantic every week. After the war had ended the company planned to relaunch the service at the earliest opportunity but it was unable to do this immediately. The loss of the *Lusitania* in May 1915, followed by the sinking of the *Justicia* ex-*Statendam*, her hinted replacement, in September 1918, had made this impossible for the foreseeable future. Nevertheless, Cunard, along with the other British companies operating on the route, found itself in a position to exploit the premium North Atlantic service to its advantage while competition was almost non-existent. In 1920 there was virtually no American presence on the run, the German threat had been eradicated for the time being, while France's Compagnie Générale Transatlantique (the French Line) was not at that time the force it was later to become.

Effort to reinstate the express service to New York was therefore paramount and to fill the gap left by the torpedoed *Lusitania*, Cunard secured the provision of the former Hamburg Amerika Line giant *Imperator*, ceded to Great Britain under the Treaty of Versailles. Initially chartered from the Shipping Controller, she was purchased outright in February 1921 in a joint purchase deal with White Star to avoid the two lines outbidding each other. For its part, White Star acquired the *Imperator's* former fleetmate, the *Bismarck*. The huge *Imperator*, ranked third in size in the world, one of the trio for which Albert Ballin, the Hamburg Amerika President, had held such high hopes, made a number of crossings for Cunard under her original name prior to embarking upon a major overhaul.

The *Imperator's* first sailing for Cunard commenced from Liverpool on 21 February 1920, making her the largest passenger liner ever to enter the River Mersey. Sailings on the New York run from Liverpool continued until the *Imperator* was transferred to the Southampton and

Cherbourg to New York route, making her first departure on 16 April 1921. At the same time the great liner experienced a change of gender as she reverted from an Emperor into a Queen and was bestowed the name *Berengaria*, honouring the consort of King Richard I. In September 1921, she was taken in hand for a long-overdue overhaul and reconditioning, including conversion of her boilers so that she could burn oil fuel. The work took eight months to complete but with evident benefits in terms of her improved performance. She resumed the Atlantic Ferry in May 1922.

Although Cunard had opened a new headquarters building at Liverpool in 1917, the company elected in the immediate postwar years to switch its United Kingdom base for the front line New York express service from the

The *Mauretania*, still the Atlantic Blue Riband holder in 1920.
David L. Williams Collection

River Mersey, the Line's birthplace, to Southampton in Hampshire. From this point onwards Southampton was confirmed as the premier British passenger port. For Cunard, the new destination allowed it to carry continental passengers routed through Cherbourg as well as American travellers destined ultimately for visits to the European mainland.

The *Berengaria* was designated as flagship of the fleet, as well as the leadship of Cunard's reinstated, though now somewhat unbalanced, three-ship express service. This constituted, besides the *Berengaria*, the smaller *Mauretania*, still the Atlantic Blue Riband record holder and which remained the fastest of the trio, and the ever-popular *Aquitania* which ranked in size between the other two and whose speed was comparable with the *Berengaria*. To maintain the service, the *Mauretania* was able to work at a reduced pace, well within her capabilities, whereas the *Aquitania* and *Berengaria* ran their engines nearer to capacity in order to sustain the required crossing times dictated by the schedule.

By way of consolation, White Star, Cunard's nearest rival, had much the same problem, having first lost the *Titanic* in collision with an iceberg in April 1912 and then her near sister *Britannic* in November 1916 after she struck a mine laid by a German submarine off Mudros. These losses had been made good by two former German ships – the Norddeutscher Lloyd *Columbus* renamed *Homeric*, and the *Bismarck* (the jointly purchased consort of the *Imperator*), which was rechristened *Majestic*. Neither of these former German vessels had completed a single commercial voyage for their original owners. As a group, with the *Olympic*, they constituted a more motley collection than their Cunard counterparts. Collectively, these Cunard and White Star ships were known as the 'Big Six'; their fortunes inevitably were closely intertwined and they dominated the transatlantic trade throughout the 1920s and early 1930s.

The *Mauretania*, then 13 years of age, had performed arduous war duties in the roles of Armed Merchant Cruiser (very briefly), hospital ship and troop transport. She had been released from military work in 1919 allowing her to

▲ The *Imperator* as a Cunard
ship prior to refit and
renaming.
David L. Williams Collection

▼ In 1920 the *Saxonia* was the
oldest surviving passenger
liner in the Cunard fleet.
Ian Allan Library

◄ The *Berengaria* in
Southampton's Ocean Dock
in the 1920s.
Ian Allan Library

The *Mauretania* was a
consistent favourite with
transatlantic travellers.
Cunard Line

The *Berengaria*, a postcard
from the 1920s. *Cunard Line*

▶ return to the North Atlantic express service, after a quick
change to Cunard colours, on 27 June of that year.
Beginning with her very first postwar sailing, the
Mauretania was placed on the new Southampton to New
York route. She, too, was in need of urgent refurbishment
for she was struggling to achieve anything like the speeds
she was capable of producing. When, on 25 July 1921, she
was severely damaged by a fire at Southampton, the
opportunity was taken during the repairs to take her in
hand for a major overhaul and conversion to oil fuel. The
larger *Aquitania*,which made her first postwar sailing two
weeks prior to the *Mauretania*, had similarly served the
country on long yeoman service and her opportunity for a
refit, on Tyneside, occurred in November 1919 when she
too had her engines adapted to burn oil fuel.

　With the *Aquitania* back in service by 1920 and the
Mauretania following her in March 1922, it took just two
more months for the Cunard Line to fully re-establish the
New York express service.

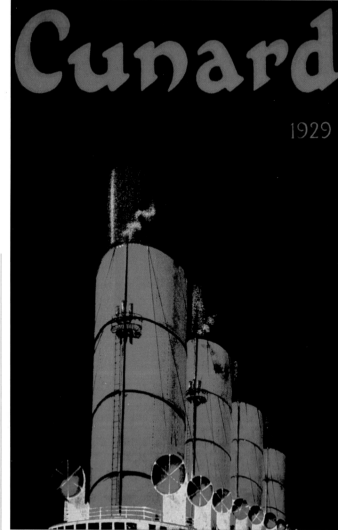

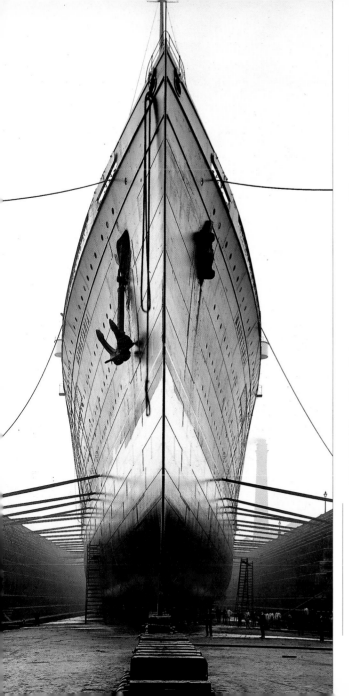

The *Mauretania's* knife-like bow, a view in drydock.
Ian Allan Library

The *Aquitania* was a popular subject with Cunard's advertising people, featuring in many of the company's posters from the 1920s and 1930s.
Cunard Line

The two 'Pretty Sisters', as they were known, the turbine-driven *Carmania* and the *Caronia*, which had quadruple-expansion steam reciprocating engines, had also survived the war. In 1914 they had been units of Cunard's express fleet. The *Carmania* was, in fact, one of the first vessels released to Cunard by the Government allowing her to make her inaugural peacetime sailing on 21 December 1918, from Liverpool to Cobh (Queenstown) and New York. The *Caronia's* first departure, on the same route, took

place a month later. Both vessels also underwent conversion to oil burning, the *Caronia* in 1920 and the *Carmania* in 1923 when her accommodation was also redistributed. From this point she could carry 425 cabin-class, 365 tourist-class and 650 third-class. Thereafter the two ships maintained Atlantic crossings on a variety of routes. The *Caronia* operated between Hamburg, Southampton and New York for a short time before being moved back to Liverpool in 1923 where she inaugurated a service to Quebec and Montreal via Belfast. A year later again remodelling of her accommodation was carried out to match that of the *Carmania*. Meanwhile, the *Carmania* had been placed temporarily on the run from Liverpool to Boston and New York. From 1926, both ships worked together again when they were placed on a new service linking London, Southampton, Le Havre and New York, with occasional calls at Plymouth. They remained on this route for the next five years.

Laid up at the end of the 1931 season, the *Caronia* and *Carmania* were disposed of for scrap within months, the former in Japan and the latter at Blyth.

In part, these frequent changes to the fleet disposition were the result of changes to the United States' policy on emigration, the quotas having been drastically cut by the American Government in 1924. Accommodation previously allocated for third-class or tourist-class traffic was upgraded and routes sought where demand existed at the higher passage rates. All this was, however, confused by the classification of fares in general and a great deal of redesignation took place as the different Atlantic operators graded broadly similar cabins in quite different classes as they endeavoured to improve their competitive position.

At this time, Cunard had no intention of introducing new vessels to the North Atlantic express service, and was apparently content to continue with the five available vessels for the foreseeable future. The elegant and beautifully appointed *Aquitania* was extremely popular, regularly carrying a near-full capacity complement of passengers.

The *Mauretania*, too, despite being 20 or so years old, had her dedicated following. In spite of her age she was now, following the reconditioning of her engines, performing better than ever. She had first taken the Atlantic Blue Riband record eastbound in November 1907 with an average speed of 23.69kt, followed by the capture of the westbound record in May 1908 with an average speed of 24.86kt. Since then she had been nibbling away at her own record times, bettering them on no fewer than seven occasions:

Westbound	September 1909	26.06kt
Eastbound	March 1908	24.42kt
	February 1909	25.28kt
	March 1909	25.61kt
	May 1909	25.70kt
	June 1909	25.88kt
	August 1924	26.16kt

Of Cunard's 'Big Three', the *Berengaria*, in spite of her size, was perhaps the least popular, though only relatively speaking. Like her former German sisters her funnel

◄◄ Another drydock picture, the larger *Aquitania* seen from the stern.
Ian Allan Library

▲ The *Aquitania* was refitted and converted to oil fuel on the River Tyne.
Cunard Line – University of Liverpool

◄ Southampton Old Docks in the 1920s. In the Ocean Dock are, on the right, the *Aquitania* (nearest) and *Berengaria* and, on the left, the *Majestic* (nearest) and *Olympic. Southern Daily Echo*

A poster by the famous marine painter Frank H. Mason showing the funnels of the *Mauretania*. *Cunard Line*

A colourful Cunard embarkation notice, featuring the funnels of either the *Mauretania* or *Aquitania*, identifying many of Cunard's ships of the 1920s. *Cunard Line*

Sister to the steam turbine *Carmania*, this is the *Caronia* which had triple-expansion steam reciprocating engines installed to permit a comparison between the two engine types. *Ian Allan Library*

Star, with no evident succession plan, was hardly an act of complacency, but it was not long before the weakness of the arrangement was exposed. Any sense of comfort that the British lines had with their dominance of the North Atlantic passenger trade was to be suddenly shattered, the rude awakening coming as early as 1927, as until then, there had been little serious competition.

The third ship of the giant Hamburg Amerika class, the *Vaterland*, had gone to the United States Lines. Renamed *Leviathan* and operated as a troopship during the closing months of World War 1, she had been comprehensively reconstructed for her return to passenger work but, operating as a single ship on what, by definition, had to be a rather infrequent if not irregular service, she was not as successful as she might otherwise have been. Added to this she was burdened by American operating costs and from the outset she sailed 'dry' as Prohibition Laws made it illegal to sell alcoholic drinks to her passengers.

The French Line had reactivated its top grade transatlantic operations with the *France*, built in 1912 and the *Paris*, completed in 1921. The French company posed a really serious threat for the first time from 1927 when it introduced the stylish *Ile de France*, renowned for her interior décor which combined modernistic concepts with traditional standards of quality. She was hugely popular right from her maiden voyage and remained so throughout the 1930s.

Within three years, Norddeutscher Lloyd too had re-entered the scene in a big way with the streamlined record-breaking pair, the *Bremen* and *Europa*. Moreover, the *Bremen* finally wrested the Atlantic Blue Riband from the

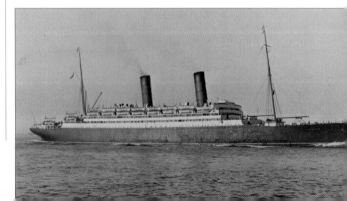

uptakes had been split to take them up the outsides of the ship, leaving a clear central vista which was exploited to the full in magnificent, long and unobscured public rooms. Yet, while the *Berengaria* did not match the *Mauretania* and *Aquitania* for patronage, she remained the most appealing of the Ballin trio, despite being the eldest and, as things turned out, she survived the longest.

The adherence to older vessels by Cunard and White

Mauretania, crossing on her maiden voyage with the new record speeds of 27.83kt westbound and 27.92kt eastbound. The *Mauretania* attempted to respond, making her best speeds ever in August 1929, at 27.65kt, but she was now a 'Grand Old Lady', a greyhound from an earlier era. However, she was to retain the distinction of having held the Atlantic Blue Riband for the longest period ever – 22 years. (The next best was the *United States* with the achievement of 17 years as the title holder from 1952 to 1969, when she was withdrawn from service.)

Last but by no means least, for the southern route from the Mediterranean, both Navigazione Generale Italiana and Lloyd Sabaudo had large, potential record-breaking new liners on the stocks in 1931.

All these new ships attracted their clientele away from the established vessels and whereas the initial impact, following their entry into service, was to decline, this still represented a significant erosion of Cunard's revenue base.

Cunard and White Star alike were galvanised into action, launching their own new ship projects. But with world depression just around the corner, the ramifications of these efforts were to totally reshape the construction of the British merchant marine as new associations were forced upon these, the nation's flagship passenger-carrying fleets.

▲ The turbine-driven *Carmania* vanquished the *Cap Polonio* during World War 1 in the only liner versus liner duel ever. *Ian Allan Library*

2. INTERMEDIATES AND THE DOMINION TRADE

Cunard had lost virtually its entire complement of Intermediate and Canadian vessels to torpedo attacks in World War 1, many of them almost new ships. The *Aurania*, which was completed in March 1917, just 11 months before she was sunk, did not make even a single commercial sailing for Cunard.

The company launched a major rebuilding programme to restore these losses. Along with replacements for cargo ship casualties, it was the largest order for ships ever placed by a single shipping company up to that time.

The first group ordered was a class of five 20,000-tonners for the Intermediate services between Liverpool or Southampton and New York or Boston. First to be completed was the *Scythia*, which made her maiden departure from Liverpool for New York on 20 August 1921. She was followed into service eight months later by

the *Samaria* whose first Atlantic crossing to Boston from Liverpool commenced on 19 April 1922. The third of the class, completing the lead batch, was the *Laconia*, honouring the 1912-built Intermediate ship of that name lost in a torpedo attack on 25 February 1917. Her maiden voyage on 25 May 1922 inaugurated the Intermediate services out of Southampton. Her début crossing was to New York but on later passages the destination alternated between New York and Boston. For some voyages, the route was also extended to Hamburg.

The *Scythia, Samaria* and *Laconia* were single-funnelled twin-screw ships with counter sterns. Their deck structures were not integral but separated into three sections – the bridge structure, the first-class accommodation area and public rooms amidships and a stern structure aft of the shelter deck. Passenger

Last of the pre-World War 1 'A' class, the *Albania*, the only vessel of her type.
Alex Duncan

accommodation was provided for 350 first-class, 350 second-class and 1,500 third-class.

The public rooms on these new Intermediate ships introduced a standard of commodiousness and comfort hitherto unknown on vessels of this class, being previously more common to those liners employed on the front-line, express mail services. Their engine installation comprised double reduction, geared steam turbines which gave them a service speed of 16kt.

Between the *Laconia* and the next of her class, the first of the new ships ordered for the Canadian routes began to enter into service. These vessels, which looked like scaled down versions of the Intermediate ships, measured around 14,000 gross tons. They too were fitted with steam turbine machinery driving twin screws, in their case delivering a service speed of 15kt. The total passenger complement of 1,700 comprised 500 first-class and 1,200 third-class. First to enter service, on the London and Southampton to Quebec and Montreal route, was the *Andania* whose maiden voyage commenced on 1 June 1922. The *Antonia* followed on 15 June 1922, sailing from Southampton, while the *Ausonia,* which came next, made her maiden voyage from Liverpool to Canada

just seven days later. Completing the lead group of four ships, a new *Aurania* made her first sailing on 9 September 1924. Initially she worked on the Liverpool to New York Intermediate service, transferring to the Dominion run out of Liverpool in 1925. During the winter months, when the St Lawrence River was frozen over, the 'A' class ships terminated at either Halifax, Nova Scotia or St John, New Brunswick.

A hybrid 'A' class ship, the *Albania*, the first ship to be completed in Cunard Line's postwar programme was in fact the last unit of the prewar 'A' class delivered in modified (utility configuration) form. She was also employed on the Canadian service out of Liverpool from 1922, her maiden voyage from Liverpool to New York having taken place on 18 January of the previous year. Smaller than the other 'A' vessels, at around 12,500 gross tons, she carried only 500 cabin-class passengers. Compared with the other four ships, however, the *Albania* had much greater cargo capacity. As the victim of circumstances, she was left as a one-off. She did not comfortably fit in with the Dominion schedules or any other service pattern for that matter, and, from 1925, she was laid up with no future in prospect as a Cunard ship.

▲ Lead ship of the new class of Intermediate steamships, the *Scythia* of 1921. *Ian Allan Library*

◄ The *Samaria* assisted by tugs. *Ian Allan Library*

Cunard had forged its operating strength and reputation well before World War 1 by offering consistent standards of accommodation and regular passage timetables on established, long-standing routes. Success was hard to come by when it deviated from these proven practices as was demonstrated in the case of the *Albania*. After five years of idleness she was sold for further service to the Italian company Libera Triestina.

In 1912, Cunard had acquired all of the shares in the Anchor Line, a company which traditionally operated out of Glasgow. While the Anchor concern was allowed to continue to function independently, quite close working relationships nevertheless developed between the two concerns. Vessels were chartered and transferred between the two, to cover periods of overhaul or when demand on either's routes dictated a need for additional tonnage, a process made all the easier in the knowledge that the quality of accommodation and standards of service were comparable.

Anchor, too, had suffered serious losses over the course of the submarine war and, to make these good, had ordered a quartet of strikingly modern 16,000-gross ton liners from Glasgow shipyards in 1919. Bearing the names *Cameronia*, *Tyrrhenia*, *Tuscania* and *California* they were among the first passenger ships to have cruiser sterns. The second of the four, the *Tyrrhenia*, was launched on 31 May 1920 but by this time she had become a Cunard vessel, the order with William Beardmore having been taken over by the parent company. Initially, commencing with her premier voyage on 13 June 1922, she operated on the Glasgow and Liverpool to Montreal route, a year later transferring to the service from Hamburg to New York.

As completed her accommodation comprised 265 first-class, 370 second-class and 1,150 third-class. In 1924 it was completely restyled, the revised layout providing for 580 cabin-class, a grade of accommodation which enjoyed standards little inferior to the former first-class but at fares closer to the old second-class, plus 1,000 third-class. Simultaneously, she was renamed *Lancastria*, her original name having proved to be something of a tongue-twister and the butt of unfavourable humour.

Two years later, the *Lancastria* was placed on a London, Le Havre, and Southampton to New York route, which she continued to work for the next six years. Threatened with similar fortunes to those of the *Albania*, if condemned to work as a lone ship on the service, Cunard chartered her former sister ship *Tuscania* to support her, although their classes of accommodation were not identical.

Back in 1923, the fourth of Cunard's new Intermediate ships had entered service, making her inaugural sailing on the Liverpool to New York route on 23 June. The *Franconia*, along with the fifth vessel of the class, named *Carinthia*, which made her début on 22 August 1925, differed in outward appearance from the earlier three ships. In the case of the *Franconia* and *Carinthia*, the main, central part of the superstructure was fabricated as a fully integrated, single construction, thus the later pair had slightly bigger tonnages.

The *Franconia* carried 221 first-class, 356 second-class and 1,266 third-class passengers. As for the *Carinthia*, whose entry into service after a gap of two years allowed for modifications to the accommodation layout in the light of operating experience, her passenger spaces were divided 240 first-class, 460 second-class and 950 third-class. By this time, all five ships of the group were operating the Liverpool to New York service. The Intermediate demand out of Southampton was satisfied by the larger volume of second- and third-class

◀◀ One of six new ships for the Canadian service, the *Andania*.
Cunard Line

◀◀ The Intermediate steamer *Lancastria*, after she had been renamed, featured in a Cunard poster.
Cunard Line

▼ Fourth of Cunard's five-ship 'Intermediate class', the *Franconia*.
Philip Rentell Collection

◀ The *Franconia's* sister ship, the *Carinthia*.
Philip Rentell Collection

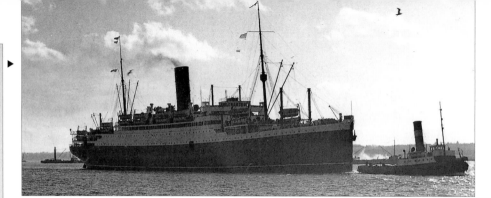

An 'A' class ship, the *Ascania,* in January 1937. *Maritime Photo Library*

The *Laconia* in the River Mersey. *Ian Allan Library*

The *Lancastria* ex-*Tyrrhenia*. *Alex Duncan*

The *Antonia*.
Ian Allan Library

The *Andania* of 1922,
second ship of the name.
Ian Allan Library

Another view of the
Carinthia.
Philip Rentell Collection

The *Franconia*.
Ian Allan Library

accommodation available on the *Aquitania, Berengaria* and *Mauretania*, with the bonus that crossing times were quicker for these passengers. From 1926 this provision was reinforced by space aboard the *Lancastria* and the chartered *Tuscania*, operating via Southampton on the London to New York service.

The final pair of the 'A' class steamers for the Dominion services were commissioned in 1925, completing Cunard's massive postwar rebuilding programme. These were the *Ascania* and *Alaunia* which made their maiden voyages respectively from Liverpool to Quebec and Montreal on 24 July 1925 and from London and Southampton to Quebec and Montreal on 22 May 1925.

The six ships of the group finally settled down, the *Andania, Antonia* and *Aurania* based primarily at Liverpool and the *Ausonia, Alaunia* and *Ascania* maintaining the southern half of the Dominion service from London and Southampton.

By the end of the 1920s, as the result of the company's major investment initiatives, Cunard was running an unrivalled fleet of 17 passenger ships on the North Atlantic, the envy of just about every other ship operator on the western ocean. Despite this enormous effort, however, the progress of events elsewhere was already threatening to overtake Cunard, significantly at the level of the prestigious, express ships which had not featured in the rebuilding programme. The stakes were high, for it was known that the overall prosperity of the fleet was to a large extent dependent on the ranking of the company's front-line ships. This had been seriously undermined by the arrival of the *Bremen* and *Europa* and risked further erosion from the newly reorganised Italia Flotta Riunite which was about to introduce two similar-sized express ships onto the 'Sunny Southern Route' from the Mediterranean. The travelling public of those days, while not fickle, could nevertheless be persuaded to transfer their allegiance to the record breakers which were in a class on their own. Their sophisticated, modern interiors, their racy lines and higher speeds contrasted with the stolid but outdated grandeur of the British 'Big Six'.

See America! Homeward by R.m.s "Queen Mary" Scotland's Pride

GLASGOW TO BOSTON AND NEW YORK

Cunard White Star

The 'A' class ship *Antonia* after the merger between Cunard and White Star, promoting trips to the United States from Glasgow, returning aboard the *Queen Mary*.
Cunard Line

Given its position as the dominant force on the North Atlantic, Cunard responded in appropriate fashion with a concept ahead of all its rivals. But the timing was hardly auspicious as the world collapsed into financial ruin following the crash of the Wall Street stock market in October 1929.

Last of the five new Intermediate ships, the *Carinthia* commissioned in 1925. *Alex Duncan*

A further two 'A' class ships, the *Aurania* in October 1936 and...

...the *Alaunia* in May 1939, close to the end of her commercial career. *Both Maritime Photo Library*

3. AMALGAMATION AND THE TWO-SHIP EXPRESS SERVICE

The story of Cunard's bid to reclaim supremacy of the North Atlantic routes goes back to 1926 when the company's directors first contemplated running the express service using only two ships instead of three, each vessel being required to make a departure from either side of the Atlantic every week. To achieve this, the vessels in question would have to be capable of 29kt service speed in order to make crossings of 4½ days' duration, leaving enough time in port for the turnaround (rebunkering, revictualling, laundry services, general cleaning and so on) and still sustain the schedule.

In turn, to carry the size of engines necessary to achieve these speeds, while accommodating sufficient passengers to make their operation viable even at reduced occupancy, vessels of at least 80,000 gross tons would have to be built.

This would be no mean undertaking. Few shipyards were capable of building such monster ships, some 50% to 60% bigger than the largest vessels then afloat, and there was also the question of costs. Equally, there were a number of logistical issues to resolve: provision of terminals capable of handling the numbers of passengers arriving and departing at one time as well as the means of getting them to and from the port of embarkation; drydocks large enough to accommodate such long liners during their annual overhauls, and so on.

All these issues and numerous others were resolved as Cunard developed the conceptual studies into firm plans. Facing stiff competition from its longstanding rival, Norddeutscher Lloyd, it had few choices. It could do nothing, of course. It could replace the existing ships with similar-sized vessels continuing the existing, three-vessel express service, or take the plunge and respond to the opposition in the most dramatic and far-seeing way possible, changing at a stroke the entire basis of contemporary North Atlantic operational thinking. Committed to remaining the biggest and best, Cunard realistically had only one option and took it, ordering the

first of a planned pair of giant new liners from the John Brown shipyard on 1 December 1930.

For four years known only by her yard number 534, probably one of the most famous three-digit numerical sequences ever, she was laid down on 27 December 1930 amid great celebration and expectation. Of course, prior to the placing of the order and the laying of the first keel plate, the bottom had fallen out of the international stock market, sending reverberations throughout the world of commerce and finance. Banks foreclosed on debtors, businesses collapsed, workers were thrown on to longer and longer 'dole' queues, everywhere was in economic ruin. For Cunard, along with other shipping operators, the numbers of passengers diminished alarmingly and revenues began to dry up, hardly the basis for funding the ambitious two-ship express project.

As if that was not all, Cunard was now facing more rivalry from its competitors. Across the English Channel, the French Line was about to commence the construction

From White Star to Cunard: the *Majestic* prior to the merger, then the world's largest liner. *Cunard Line*

of a new ship equal in size to the 534, although it was not clear whether this was the first step towards instituting a rival two-ship service. Meanwhile, back at home, the White Star Line had ordered its own giant new flagship from Harland & Wolff, Belfast, a new diesel-electric-powered *Oceanic*. First conceived in August 1926, the 60,000-gross ton vessel was to form the key element of its programme of renascence, replacing that company's equally-ageing premier ships.

The story of how all these related issues unfolded as the early 1930s advanced, elevating ocean liner travel and the affairs of the major operating players to the newspaper headlines, is now almost legendary. Being central to the restoration of Cunard's glorious position of champion of the North Atlantic it is related here in a somewhat condensed form.

Faced with the unremitting reality of the international financial situation, Cunard was obliged to suspend the construction of the 534 in December 1931, leaving the folk

of Clydeside to endure one of the bleakest yuletides in living memory. Over in Northern Ireland, the *Oceanic* had not progressed far beyond the laying of her keel structure, started on 28 June 1928, when she too was stopped amid intense speculation as to whether it was merely a postponement or a complete abandonment of the project. If anything, White Star was in even more dire straits than Cunard.

Back in 1902, White Star had been absorbed into the International Mercantile Marine combine as the American

MAJESTIC

◀◀ Against the New York skyline, the *Majestic* now promoting her new owners. *Cunard Line*

◀ Three famous red Cunard funnels. It can only be one ship – the *Queen Mary*. *Cunard Line*

industrialist J. Pierpont Morgan sought to dominate the Atlantic by the simple expedient of buying up and owning every operator on the run, irrespective of its nationality. A quarter of a century on, in the approach to the world's worst depression, the IMM was in the process of disposing of its foreign assets and the shares of the Oceanic Steam Navigation Co (White Star) were bought up by the Royal Mail. But Royal Mail was, itself, not well equipped to weather the turbulence of the Great Depression and continuation with new buildings on the scale of the proposed *Oceanic* was dubious to say the least.

As for Cunard, it had turned to the British Government

The *Olympic*, the only
surviving unit of the
ambitious trio of luxurious
giants conceived by White
Star back in 1909.
Tom Rayner Collection

One of the pair of new
motorships built by White
Star in the early 1930s, the
Britannic on the slipway at
Belfast prior to her launch.
Ian Allan Library

▲ for help but, fearing this would trigger a similar demand
from White Star, the granting of loan aid had been made
conditional upon the two companies merging into one
concern. Agreement between the parties was finally
reached in February 1934 and Cunard White Star Ltd was
formed, Cunard contributing 62% of the equity and White
Star 38%. Resulting from the amalgamation, the company
▶ had an enormous fleet of passenger ships and the first step
was to dispose of tonnage for which gainful employment
could no longer be provided, principally White Star ships.
The casualties included the veteran *Adriatic*, the *Calgaric,
Albertic* and *Homeric*, all sold for breaking up, and the
Ceramic transferred to Shaw Savill for continued operation
on the Australian service run. The *Olympic* survived until
September 1935 when she was sold for scrapping at
Jarrow. The same year saw the once proud *Mauretania*,
disposed of for the same fate, leaving Southampton for the
last time bound for the breaker's yard at Rosyth on 1 July
1935. Another casualty, which further reduced the
remnants of the White Star fleet, involved the relatively
new *Doric*. Severely damaged in a collision on 5 September
1935, she was considered to be beyond economic recovery
and she too was sold for demolition.

   This left Cunard White Star with the *Aquitania, Berengaria*
and *Majestic* as the front-line ships pending the
introduction of the giant ship completing on Clydebank

which had received the name *Queen Mary*, not *Victoria* as speculated, when she was finally launched on 26 September 1934. In itself this was a remarkable piece of excellent public relations and diplomacy. It identified the new vessel with the consort of the ruling monarch, engaging the patriotic support of the entire nation while avoiding the controversy of bias that could have resulted from a name ending in 'ia' (Cunard tradition) or 'ic' (White Star tradition). Apart from the express ships, the other members of the combined fleet were the six 'A' class vessels, the five 'Scythia' class Intermediates, the *Lancastria* and White Star's two new motorships *Britannic* and *Georgic*, a total of 17 ships.

The *Queen Mary* made her long-anticipated maiden voyage from Southampton on 27 May 1936, having given a hint of what she was capable of during speed trials over the Skelmorlie measured mile, off the Isle of Arran in the Firth of Clyde. During the protracted delay to her construction, the French Line had stolen the march on Cunard. Its marvellous new liner *Normandie* projected a flamboyant modernity of style which exuded a Gallic flair in marked contrast to the British ship's bold rake and powerful presence which suggested she was made of rather sterner stuff. The turbo-electric-powered *Normandie* took the Atlantic Blue Riband immediately, clipping a comfortable margin off the best times of the *Bremen* and *Rex* which had held the record since the eclipsing of the *Mauretania*. But the *Queen Mary* was not trying, yet! In August 1936, on her fifth round voyage she took the *Normandie's* crown, with speeds westbound of 30.14kt and eastbound of 30.63kt. The latter was all the more remarkable for she had completed the first ever sub-four-day crossing of the Atlantic by sea. In precise terms it had taken her 3 days 23hr 57min.

That was not the end of the competition though, and the continuing contest between the British and French flagships only served to give both companies and ocean travel as a whole the kind of publicity that was sorely needed to lift them out of the Depression. The *Normandie* regained the honours in 1937 only to lose them again to the *Queen Mary*, permanently this time, in 1938. The *Queen*

Mary's best ever crossing times, recorded that August, were 30.99kt westbound and 31.69kt eastbound.

The quality and finery of the *Queen Mary's* interiors was all that might be expected of a superliner, the new British flagship. They were superb – 'Grand Luxe' to use a popular expression of the time – and exhibited the best of British craftsmanship and the most creative of British decorative design. She catered for almost 2,700 passengers in three classes. In a master-stroke, giving her an immediate competitive advantage, Cunard graded her accommodation as first, cabin and tourist rather than first, second and third. Her engines were massive single-reduction geared steam turbines driving quadruple screws. She could achieve a maximum speed of the order of 32kt.

The introduction of the *Queen Mary* had rendered the old *Majestic* surplus to requirements, her even older sister *Berengaria* being preferred for retention along with the *Aquitania* for which there was no suggestion of retirement

The *Georgic* arriving in the Mersey. *Ian Allan Library*

Inset:
The *Queen Mary* at speed –
a classic postcard of the
celebrated liner.
David L. Williams Collection

◀◀ 'Visit America – Cunard White Star': evoking the Jazz era, this card reveals some of the many design possibilities afforded to ocean travel publicists at that time.
Cunard Line

◀ 'America this Year by RMS *Queen Mary*'. Promotions aimed at encouraging greater travel abroad, in Cunard's case to boost their transatlantic business, did not reach the wider population until the 1970s and 1980s in the age of air travel, long after the Atlantic Ferry had passed into history.
Cunard Line

at this point. In May 1936, the very month of the *Queen Mary's* maiden voyage, the already inactive *Majestic* was sold for breaking up but in a last-minute reprieve she was purchased by the Admiralty and converted into the stationary Artificers Training Ship HMS *Caledonia*.

Later that year, in December, the second phase of Cunard's planned two-ship weekly service was activated with the laying down of the *Queen Elizabeth* in the same

Clyde shipyard.

The intention was for the *Berengaria* to make way for the *Queen Elizabeth* when she was commissioned in 1940, while a third, smaller ship ordered from Cammell Laird, Birkenhead would provide cover for the two 'Queens' in place of the *Aquitania*. For the rest of the time the third new ship would maintain a London, Le Havre, Southampton and New York service in consort with the

The first docking in the King George V Graving Dock at Southampton where the *Queen Mary* was prepared for her sea trials.
Ian Allan Library

two remaining White Star motorships. These plans were thwarted, however, when the old *Berengaria*, now well beyond her prime, started to develop serious mechanical and electrical problems. A serious outbreak of fire on board while she was berthed at New York on 3 March 1938 led the United States' authorities to refuse to issue her passenger clearance certificate. Ignominiously, she sailed home empty and, on her arrival at Southampton, she was immediately laid up prior to disposal for scrap in the October, leaving an awkward gap in the ranks.

Bigger and more serious matters than this were conspiring to deny to Cunard the opportunity of fully implementing its ambitious Atlantic express service. Ironically, it was just as the passenger trade was perking up, lifting the gloom of the early 1930s and with Cunard's fortunes riding the crest of the wave, its popularity having never been higher, that the storm clouds of impending war began to gather once more over Europe.

The new medium-sized liner was christened *Mauretania* when she was launched on 28 July 1938, to commemorate the recently paid-off record breaker. She entered service on 17 June 1939, making her first crossing from Liverpool to New York, returning to Southampton via Cherbourg. Like the *Aquitania*, a quarter of a century earlier, she was to experience only the briefest period of commercial operation before the outbreak of hostilities was to interrupt this work for more than six years. The *Mauretania's* smart and stylish accommodation marked a

further enhancement to the standards of cabins, public rooms and general facilities provided for passengers of all grades by Cunard. Though somewhat slower than the 'Queens' her single-reduction geared turbines gave her the creditable service speed of 23kt. At 35,738 gross tons she became the largest liner to enter the Port of London when she docked in the King George V Graving Dock in August 1939.

On 28 September 1938, the *Queen Elizabeth* had been launched at the John Brown shipyard, also honouring the Queen Consort of the ruling monarch. Optimistically, she was painted in Cunard colours for the occasion but, by the time she was nearing completion, war had been declared on Germany in response to the invasion of Poland. There was no longer any prospect of her entering the service for which she had been destined for the foreseeable future. Overpainted in naval grey, the world's largest liner secretively and solitarily headed out across the Atlantic for the first time on 26 February 1940. To distract enemy attention, all the outward indications were deliberately designed to give the impression that she was bound for Southampton and drydocking. Instead, after 'silent running' at high speed for five days, she arrived in New York. Conversion into a troopship would soon follow. Together with the *Queen Mary*, and supported by the endeavours of all the other Cunard White Star ships, she was about to write another illustrious chapter in the company's history.

Looking every inch a champion, the magnificent *Queen Mary* flat out on a trial run off the Isle of Arran, Firth of Clyde.
Ian Allan Library

In the Solent in 1938, the *Queen Mary* inward bound to Southampton after she had recovered the Blue Riband from the *Normandie*. *Ian Allan Library*

The second *Mauretania* enters the water at the Cammell Laird shipyard, Birkenhead, on 28 July 1938. *Ian Allan Library*

The elegant *Mauretania*, ready to enter service in 1939. The outbreak of war three months later curtailed her commercial operations for over six years.
Ian Allan Library

The *Queen Elizabeth* stands out against the Glasgow skyline immediately prior to her launch.
Cunard Line – University of Liverpool Archives

4. CRUISING IN THE DEPRESSION YEARS

Almost from the first opportunity after the total resumption of its full range of passenger services in the early 1920s, Cunard introduced off-peak cruise excursions. It has to be said, though, that certain of these pleasure trips were extensive affairs more realistically directed at a minority of very wealthy travellers.

Beginning with the *Laconia* and *Samaria* in their first season, Cunard offered the opportunity to make a round-the-world cruise calling at more than 30 ports, the former sailing east about, the latter heading in a westbound direction. Each voyage lasted through the long winter months from November 1922 into February 1923, starting from New York and taking in visits to Cuba, the American west coast, Japan, China, Hong Kong, the Philippines, India, Egypt, Italy and the United Kingdom, the sequence depending on which way the ship was making its circumnavigation. The passage took the ships through both the Suez and Panama Canals and included a variety of shore excursions such as to Peking from Shanghai, to Luxor to see the ancient Egyptian antiquities, across India via Benares linking the port of Calcutta and Bombay, as well as to London. An extremely ambitious option on a later *Franconia* cruise provided for a trans-Asian diversion for more daring participants. This involved leaving the ship at Yokohama and going overland via Manchuria, Siberia and Russia to Europe where a final transatlantic crossing from Southampton or Cherbourg returned the brave souls making such an intrepid excursion back to New York.

With a maximum of 450 passengers on these long-haul cruises, they were styled as 'Club'-type affairs; for unlike the majority of the other cruises available at that time, the emphasis was unashamedly on exclusiveness.

So successful were these ventures, though, that Cunard continued to make round-the-world cruises intermittently available right through to the last summer of peace before World War 2. Long before today's widespread and intensive cruising trade came into being, such circumnavigations

R.M.S. "HOMERIC," 33,526 Tons

SAILING FROM

SOUTHAMPTON AND CHERBOURG TO NEW YORK

In conjunction with the R.M.S. "MAJESTIC," 56,000 Tons (the Largest Steamer in the World), and the R.M.S. "OLYMPIC," 46,439 Tons

MAINTAINING A WEEKLY EXPRESS MAIL SERVICE

◄ The *Homeric* had been a dedicated cruise liner since June 1932. She survived for less than a year after the amalgamation between Cunard and White Star. *David L. Williams Collection*

were not only exceptional but almost legendary, appealing to the discerning traveller of that era who was fortunate enough to have both the time to spare and the necessary financial standing to afford the fares. Not that all the

'Sixteen Thousand Miles of Sunshine' – poster promoting the *Laconia's* winter cruise from Liverpool and Southampton to Africa, South America and the Caribbean in January 1938. *Cunard Line*

Bill of fare for the *Franconia's* 1939 world cruise. *Cunard Line*

Dressed overall, the yacht-like cruise liner *Mauretania* off Cowes, Isle of Wight. *World Ship Photo Library*

berths cost a king's ransom. A limited amount of accommodation was set aside on E-deck for the relatively less affluent passenger at a rate of $1,350 all-in, itself a significant reduction on the advertised minimum fare of $3,000. This, nevertheless, equals a cost today of more than £10,000, allowing for inflation and the reduced pound/dollar exchange rates that have prevailed since 1945.

Comparable world cruises were made over the next 15 years, annually from 1925 to 1939, by the *Franconia* and *Carinthia*, the last ships of the 'Scythia' class, both of which were designed with cruising as well as regular services in mind. The *Carinthia's* circumnavigation of 1933 took in 40 ports. On her world cruise of 1938, the *Franconia* steamed 41,727 miles and called at 37 ports. The next year she

ROUND THE WORLD CRUISE, 1939

IN THE

PALATIAL WORLD - CRUISING LINER

" FRANCONIA " (20,000 TONS)

ITINERARY

Port		Miles	Arrive				Sail			
SOUTHAMPTON	...	—				—	Sat.,	Dec. 24	—
NEW YORK	...	3,000	Mon.,	Jan.	2.	—	Thur.,	Jan. 5,	00.05 am
PORT OF SPAIN	...	1,932	Tues.,	,,	10.	6.00 am	Tues.,	,, 10,	2.00 pm
RIO DE JANEIRO	...	3,136	Thur.,	,,	19.	7.00 am	Fri.,	,, 20,	Midnight
BUENOS AIRES	...	1,142	Tues.,	,,	24.	6.00 am	Wed.,	,, 25,	6.00 pm
MONTEVIDEO	...	125	Thur.,	,,	26.	7.00 am	Thur.,	,, 26,	Noon
CAPETOWN	...	3,649	Sun.,	Feb.	5.	Noon	Thur.,	Feb. 9,	5.00 pm
PORT ELIZABETH	...	422	Sat.,	,,	11.	6.00 am	Sat.,	,, 11,	5.00 pm
DURBAN	...	396	Mon.,	,,	13.	6.00 am	Thur.,	,, 16,	5.00 pm
ZANZIBAR	...	1,607	Tues.,	,,	21.	6.00 am	Tues.,	,, 21,	6.00 pm
MOMBASA	...	132	Wed.,	,,	22.	6.00 am	Wed.,	,, 22,	5.00 pm
PORT VICTORIA	...	969	Sat.,	,,	25.	8.30 am	Sat.,	,, 25,	1.30 pm
BOMBAY	...	1,752	Thur.,	Mar.	2.	8.30 am	Thur.,	Mar. 9,	6.00 pm
COLOMBO	...	889	Sun.,	,,	12.	6.00 am	Tues.,	,, 14,	6.00 pm
BELAWAN DELI	...	1,240	Sat.,	,,	18.	6.00 am	Sat.,	,, 18,	6.00 pm
PENANG	...	145	Sun.,	,,	19.	8.00 am	Mon.,	,, 20,	5.00 pm
SINGAPORE	...	393	Tues.,	,,	21.	8.00 am	Tues.,	,, 21,	6.00 pm
PAKNAM	...	811	Fri.,	,,	24.	2.00 am	Fri.,	,, 24,	9.00 pm
TOURANE	...	1,134	Tues.,	,,	28.	5.00 am	Tues.,	,, 28,	7.00 pm
HONG KONG	...	519	Thur.,	,,	30.	7.00 am	Fri.,	,, 31,	5.00 pm
MANILA	...	630	Sun.,	April	2.	11.00 am	Mon.,	April 3,	2.00 am
BATAVIA	...	1,562	Fri.,	,,	7.	8.00 am	Sat.,	,, 8,	2.30 pm
SEMARANG	...	236	Sun.,	,,	9.	6.00 am	Sun.,	,, 9,	2.00 pm
PADANG BAY (Bali)	...	423	Tues.,	,,	11.	6.00 am	Wed.,	,, 12,	5.00 pm
KUPANG (Timor)	...	503	Fri.,	,,	14.	6.00 am	Fri.,	,, 14,	5.00 pm
PORT DARWIN	...	475	Sun.,	,,	16.	6.00 am	Sun.,	,, 16,	4.00 pm
PORT MORESBY (Papua)	...	1,081	Thur.,	,,	20.	1.00 am	Thur.,	,, 20,	9.00 pm
FILA (New Hebrides)	...	1,340	Mon.,	,,	24.	1.00 pm	Mon.,	,, 24,	6.00 pm
NOUMEA (New Caledonia)	...	328	Wed.,	,,	26.	6.00 am	Wed.,	,, 26,	Noon
SUVA (Fiji)	...	730	Fri.,	,,	28.	2.00 pm	Sat.,	,, 29,	3.00 am
NUKUALOFA (Friendly Is.)	...	436	Sun.,	,,	30.	10.00 am	Sun.,	,, 30,	5.00 pm
PAGO PAGO (E. Samoa)	...	490	Mon.,	May	1.	6.00 am	Mon.,	May 1,	6.00 pm
APIA (W. Samoa)	...	88	Tues.,	,,	2.	5.00 am	Tues.,	,, 2,	1.00 pm
HONOLULU	...	2,262	Mon.,	,,	8.	4.00 pm	Tues.,	,, 16,	4.00 pm
SAN FRANCISCO	...	2,091	Mon.,	,,	15.	10.00 am	Tues.,	,, 16,	10.00 am
BALBOA	...	3,246	Mon.,	,,	22.	6.00 am	Thur.,	,, 25,	Noon
CRISTOBAL	...	44	Thur.,	,,	25.	8.00 pm		No stop	
NEW YORK	...	1,972	Wed.,	,,	31.	6.00 am	Fri.,	June 2,	
LIVERPOOL	...	3,000	Mon.,	,,	12.				
		44,333							

Subject to Alteration

RATES FROM **410 GNS.**

(Including Standard Shore Excursions).

This Winter's Greatest Cruise

16,000 miles of sunshine

CANARY ISLES · AFRICA (Senegal)
STH. AMERICA · PANAMA · WEST
INDIES · BAHAMAS · FLORIDA
MADEIRA

by the favourite cruising liner
'LACONIA'
20,000 tons

From Liverpool	From Southampton
Jan. 26	Jan. 28

52 days from 100 gns

New World Rivieras—Florida, California, Gulf Coast, Nassau, Bermuda, Jamaica. Through bookings via New York at inclusive rates

Write for illustrated folder to your local agent or Cunard White Star Ltd., Liverpool, London

Cunard White Star

made the last such voyage prior to World War 2 which was well supported despite the deteriorating political situation. Lasting from January to June 1939 it afforded her lucky passengers the opportunity in those last days of peace to take in the delights of some 38 destinations around the world, many of which would never be the same again, soon to be changed beyond all recognition. Not all of Cunard's cruises were in this league, nor were they all operated in such auspicious and prosperous circumstances. Throughout the period from 1925 all five of the 'Scythia' class ships made off-season winter cruises of varying durations, the West Indies and Bermuda being popular destinations from New York. For the most part, this constituted the bulk of Cunard's cruise effort at that time, for the company was not then naturally associated with cruise travel.

After the Wall Street crash the trading situations on the scheduled service routes dramatically worsened and in the bleak years of the early 1930s Cunard switched many of its vessels to long periods of cruising as the only means of ensuring their survival. This was not limited to the smaller vessels of the fleet either, for continued operation depended on making revenues in any way possible.

The *Lancastria*, which had not properly settled in the London to New York service operated with her former Anchor Line consort, was switched increasingly to short cruises from Liverpool, full-time from 1936.

In 1931, the ageing *Mauretania* was withdrawn from the express mail service and transferred to cruise work, in effect marking the end of her career as a transatlantic liner. As if to reinforce the permanence of the change, she was repainted with a white hull which not only befitted the nature of her new role, operating in the warmer temperatures of the Mediterranean and Caribbean, but also gave her a sleek, yacht-like appearance. Her new lease of life carried her through to 1935 but then, surplus to the new Cunard White Star Co's requirements, she was laid up at Southampton prior to being disposed of for scrap. The final departure of this well-loved and fondly remembered greyhound of the Atlantic, was a sad affair, witnessed by thousands of adoring shoreside spectators who took the time to pay their respects at her last farewell.

Another of the front-line Cunarders which was also struggling in the depths of the Great Depression was the *Berengaria*. In what seemed to amount to desperate measures she was sent on £50 set-fare 'booze' cruises from New York into Canadian waters, exploiting the continuing American yearning for alcoholic liquor in the days before the repeal of the Prohibition laws.

The *Berengaria* too was never quite the same ship on the Atlantic service after this undignified diversion. She followed on her way to the breaker's yard in 1938 without ever being fully restored to front-line duties.

Recognising the value of the cruising business as a money spinner in this difficult period, the ships of the 'Scythia' class were increasingly diverted into this work from the early 1930s. The *Laconia*, which had started it all in 1922, was frequently occupied cruising between 1930 and 1939. From 1934 the *Samaria* did much the same, regularly operating a programme of summer cruises from

▼ An unusual sight at New York, the white-hulled *Mauretania* makes a call during a cruise.
Ian Allan Library

The *Carinthia* made cruises in the 1920s, painted black and...

...in the 1930s, painted white, a colour which enhanced the *Carinthia's* graceful lines.
Both Philip Rentell Collection

London. The *Franconia* and *Carinthia*, to which fell the bulk of the cruising details, were painted white, like the *Mauretania*, giving them an elegance of style which they never really had when their hulls were painted black.

The *Lancastria* too was given cruising livery as if to acknowledge that this was her full-time role for the foreseeable future. She was pointedly marketed to appeal to workers, still lucky enough to have a job, offering holidays of a lifetime at unbelievably cheap prices. For example, £18 for a two-week cruise to the Mediterranean or, from £23, a 22-day cruise taking in Gibraltar, Tangier, Lisbon and the Atlantic isles, the price including all 'standard' shore excursions.

Cruise fares generally in this period were rock-bottom, representing exceptional value for those who had the spare cash, as well as the opportunity to take advantage. In the final season prior to the outbreak of war, the *Laconia* offered a 52-day excursion to South America, the Caribbean and Florida from 100 guineas (£105). Similarly, fares for the *Franconia's* last world cruise started from 410 guineas (£430) although these were still hardly the bill of

fare of the man in the street.

The hint of egalitarianism that had crept into the cruise business during the 1930s would not resurface again until the cruising boom of the 1970s and 1980s. After World War 2, the word 'cruise' in holiday brochures and on posters in travel agents' windows would again be appended with the adjective 'luxury' with prices befitting this distinguishing accolade.

The *Franconia* was another Cunarder that spent long periods cruising in the 1930s.
Philip Rentell Collection

The *Aquitania* – cruising in the Depression years became a regular activity for her. *Cunard Line*

Dressed overall for the Coronation Fleet Review in May 1937, by this time the *Lancastria* was more or less permanently engaged on inexpensive ocean tours. *Ian Allan Library*

The *Aquitania* on the same occasion. She too was employed extensively on short duration cruises from New York during the 1930s. *Maritime Photo Library*

A celebrated Cunard cruise liner over two decades, the *Laconia*. *Tom Rayner Collection*

A marvellous view of the *Carinthia* in cruising colours in the River Mersey. *Ian Allan Library*

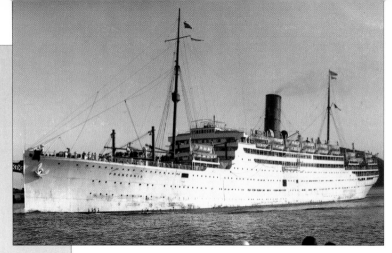

The *Franconia* while cruising in the 1930s. In 1931 she was chartered to the Furness Bermuda Line for five months after their new ship *Bermuda* was ravaged by fire at Hamilton, Bermuda. *Alex Duncan*

The *Mauretania's* final departure from Southampton, bound for ship breakers at Rosyth, on 1 July 1935. Her last transatlantic voyage from New York had begun on 26 September 1934, the same day as the *Queen Mary* was launched at Clydebank. *Southern Daily Echo*

The *Berengaria* at Southampton. Her career came to an abrupt, even premature end in October 1938. *Maritime Photo Library*

5. AUXILIARY SERVICE IN THE WAR AT SEA

The dominance of the ocean sea-lanes in peacetime, which Cunard and other British shipping companies had achieved, gave the nation a military advantage in wartime beyond measure. No other country engaged in the fighting of World War 2 was able to muster the same quantities of passenger vessels as Great Britain, which allowed the transportation of vast armies of men all over the globe, both its own and its allies'. And those ships not employed in this fashion were engaged to supplement the nation's naval forces, providing additional escort and patrol capabilities.

Any description of Cunard's participation in the war at sea during World War 2 is bound to present the phenomenal contribution made by the *Queen Mary* and *Queen Elizabeth* as its highlight. Between them, after conversion to troopships at Sydney, these two giant liners steamed over a million miles, ferrying first Anzac troops to Great Britain and the Middle East and, later, from May 1943, transporting GIs across the Atlantic in the build-up to the invasion of Europe.

They sailed independently, relying on their speed as their best protection from submarine attack. In the event, not one submarine was sighted by either vessel over the course of the war, nor for that matter was a single enemy aircraft. Although each was equipped with some 30 or more guns of different sizes, neither vessel was called upon to fire them in anger.

In total the 'Queens' carried some 1,243,538 Allied servicemen in the six years of conflict, fighting-power on a scale that it has been calculated had the effect of shortening the war by weeks or even months and, as a consequence, saving thousands of lives. Of course, with their enormous capacity they could carry a full division of troops, as graphically portrayed in a number of now famous photographs showing their crowded decks. With that in mind, the magnificent service provided by the crews of the 'Queens', catering, laundering and generally

The second *Mauretania* in grey paint as a troopship. *Imperial War Museum – A 28105*

taking care of these many men, also deserves recognition.

Clearly, there were enormous risks involved in transporting such large numbers of troops unescorted, up to 20,000 in a single voyage. The scale of the disaster, had either of the 'Queens' been sunk with nowhere near sufficient lifeboats, does not bear thinking about. Their many safe passages owed a great deal to careful route planning by the Admiralty and the United States Navy, the use of identical or similar courses being carefully avoided. It helped, too, to know that the Germans preferred to concentrate U-boat attacks on slow-moving convoys.

The gamble paid off and they both came through the war unscathed. That is with the exception of an unfortunate incident which involved the *Queen Mary* on 2 October 1942, a tragic accident which was the only blemish in her otherwise impeccable war record. While approaching Scotland, some 20 miles from the sadly appropriately-named Bloody Foreland, she rammed and sliced in two the light cruiser HMS *Curacao* which had been directed to escort the troopship into port. The cruiser sank within minutes, with the loss of 338 officers and men, the *Queen Mary* being obliged to continue from the scene full speed ahead leaving the few survivors struggling in the water. Any other action, no matter how much more preferable, would have exposed her 15,000 American troops to the danger of torpedo attack. The disaster occurred as the two vessels were manoeuvring close together in foggy conditions, but the precise circumstances which led to the collision were clouded in confusion. An enquiry after the war totally exonerated the master and officers of the *Queen Mary.*

Cunard's wartime achievements, viewed as a balanced whole, were the product of the entire fleet of passenger ships and not just the two 'Queens'. All the other vessels made equally valuable, if unsung, contributions to the Allied cause, steaming huge distances around the world without the benefit of the level of servicing and overhaul which would have routinely been associated with just a fraction of this effort while on peacetime schedules.

The wonderful, old *Aquitania* became one of the few large liners to perform military service twice in her career. Having been destined, originally, for retirement in 1940 on the *Queen Elizabeth's* entry into service, she instead clocked up an impressive half a million miles of ocean steaming, equivalent to 20 circumnavigations of the Earth, carrying 338,701 Allied soldiers.

The *Aquitania* participated in the early trooping convoys from Australia. In April 1940 she was part of one of the

greatest convoys ever mustered for the transportation of troops from Sydney to Africa. With her were the Canadian Pacific ships *Empress of Britain, Empress of Canada* and *Empress of Asia,* along with her fleetmates *Queen Mary, Queen Elizabeth* and the new *Mauretania* as well as the Dutch liner *Nieuw Amsterdam.*

When the Japanese attacked Pearl Harbour in December 1941 she was located in that region of the oceans, a far cry from her normal sphere of operation but fortunately not too close to the action. Continuing her cautious return home across the Pacific she became the largest liner ever to call at Hawaii when she entered the devastated naval base at Pearl Harbour for a brief replenishment call.

The new *Mauretania* also saw service as a troopship, converted for this work at Sydney after a brief period of idleness at Liverpool and New York. She had an exciting voyage out to Australia via Bilbao, San Francisco and Honolulu, tracked for much of the way by the enemy and having to evade concentrations of U-boats that were known to be laying in wait for her. Like the *Aquitania,* she amassed more than 500,000 sea miles over the course of her war duties, first criss-crossing the Indian Ocean, then working the Atlantic with American and Canadian troops and, finally, serving in the Pacific theatre. One of her wartime voyages, of 28,662 nautical miles duration, took

her right round the world, taking 82 days to complete. During the course of this epic voyage she established a speed record for the crossing time from Fremantle, Australia to Durban, South Africa. The 4,000-mile distance was covered in 8 days and 19hr at an average speed of 21.06kt, although she was never intended to be an exceptionally fast ship. Despite this and the fact that her engines had received scant attention for six years, she achieved an even more impressive turn of speed in 1945, making the passage from Bombay to the United Kingdom via the Cape at an average of 23.4kt.

The smaller ships of the 'A' class, with the exception of the *Antonia*, initially served as Armed Merchant Cruisers, a

▲ Lying at anchor in Gourock Bay on 21 May 1942, the *Queen Mary* embarks troops from tenders.
Imperial War Museum – A 9433

◄ Bolstering the forces fighting in the western desert, the *Queen Elizabeth* at anchor off a Middle East port on 22 July 1942. She was delivering reinforcements after a record-breaking run from the United Kingdom via the Cape. On the return leg she conveyed German prisoners to Great Britain.
Imperial War Museum – E 14696

◄ HMS *Wayland* ex-*Antonia*, Auxiliary Fleet Repair Ship at Greenock on 23 December 1942.
Imperial War Museum – A 13548

role more befitting their size and manoeuvrability, all
commissioned in the autumn of 1939. The *Andania* along
with the *Aurania* was deployed patrolling in the Orkney
and Shetlands sea area with vessels of other companies
that were not normally to be seen in such cold northern
climes. While performing these duties, on 16 June 1940,
the *Andania* was sunk by the submarine *UA1* when
southeast of Reykjavik, Iceland, fortunately without loss of
life.

June 1940 was a particularly bad month for Cunard,
three of its ships being lost over the course of 10 days. On
7 June, the *Carinthia*, which had also been converted into
an Armed Merchant Cruiser in October 1939, was
torpedoed off the Irish coast by the *U46*, four members of
her crew being killed. Ten days later, in the most
calamitous Allied shipping loss of the entire war, the
Lancastria was sunk by German bombers off St Nazaire
during the evacuation of British troops from France. In the
frantic circumstances surrounding the withdrawal, with
enemy forces rapidly advancing, she embarked a huge
number of persons, the precise number not recorded in all

the chaos. Some reports say that as many as 9,000 soldiers
and escaping civilians boarded her but the actual figure is
believed to be nearer to 5,500. Shortly after completing the
embarkation and making ready to weigh anchor and set
sail from Charpentier Roads, the evacuation area came
under attack from German warplanes. In the course of the
third wave of the attack, four bombs struck the *Lancastria*,
one exploding deep within her, causing her to sink rapidly.
Although two lifeboats were launched, there was little that
could be done in the very brief time available to effect a
rescue on the scale that was needed. After just 20 minutes,
the stricken *Lancastria* rolled over onto her port side, then
capsized completely before sinking bow first. Despite the
efforts of numerous small craft, picking up survivors from
the water, an estimated 3,000 persons perished including
66 known casualties from her crew. The official figure for
the number rescued was 2,477. The sinking of the
Lancastria was the worst British maritime disaster from
both the World Wars.

Of the other ships of the 'A' class, the *Alaunia*, *Ascania*
and *Ausonia* were also engaged as Armed Merchant

hand by the Admiralty for full conversion into Base Repair Ships, the last named rechristened HMS *Artifex*. The *Antonia*, renamed HMS *Wayland*, had already been converted in this fashion some time earlier, being first commissioned in 1940. These were not reversible conversions, so although none fell victim to enemy action, they nevertheless constituted four more lost ships from Cunard's point of view. The remaining 'A' ship, the *Ascania*, reverted to troopship duties from 1942 only to be taken over again for a naval role in 1943, serving out the war as an Infantry Landing Ship.

Apart from the unfortunate *Carinthia*, only one other of the Intermediate ships was commissioned as an Armed Merchant Cruiser, this being the *Laconia*. From 1941 she was released from naval work and adapted for the transportation of troops along the lines of her sister ships *Franconia*, *Scythia* and *Samaria* which had been so engaged all along. The *Laconia* survived as a troopship for just over a year, falling prey to a torpedo attack launched by *U156* on 12 September 1942 in another of the notorious incidents which occurred during the sea war. At the time of the sinking the *Laconia* was bound for England from Suez via the Cape with a large complement of 3,254 persons of which 1,793 were Italian prisoners of war. When about 800 miles southwest of Freetown, in the South Atlantic, the U-boat made its attack, later surfacing after the liner had sunk, to take prisoners. Discovering the true nature of the *Laconia's* occupants the commander of the *U156* summoned other nearby U-boats to the scene in order to mount a rescue, exposing his vessel to air attack. Inevitably, this occurred as four of the submarines, including the *U156*, were towing lifeboats on the surface. This was despite the fact that they were flying the flag of the Red Cross. Ultimately, the survivors, about 1,000 in total, comprising Allied seamen and guards as well as PoWs, were transhipped to surface vessels and conveyed to Casablanca. Subsequent to the event, which came to be known as 'The *Laconia* Incident', Admiral Dönitz, Commander-in-Chief of the Kriegsmarine, issued an order instructing U-boat captains to refrain from making rescue attempts in the future. On the face of it the directive conflicted with the

natural code of the sea and was considered, in the circumstances, as amounting to a war crime. Dönitz was tried for this at the Nuremburg War Crimes Trials in 1946 but was acquitted of the charge.

Two other vessels from the Cunard White Star fleet should be mentioned here, the motorships *Britannic* and *Georgic*. Both were requisitioned for troop-carrying work, providing sterling service in this capacity. The *Britannic* survived the war intact but the *Georgic* barely survived a bombing attack at Port Tewfik (Taufiq) on the Suez Canal on 14 July 1941 which left her beached and ablaze from end to end. Despite the extent of the damage it was decided that the vessel should be salvaged and repaired. Once refloated and patched-up sufficiently to make her seaworthy, the *Georgic* was slowly towed home, making calls at Port Sudan and Karachi, where further running repairs were carried out. She arrived at Liverpool, her home port, on 1 March 1943 whereupon she was transferred to Belfast for complete reconstruction from the hull upwards by her builders.

In December 1944 the liner reappeared, ready to resume duties, but she was a shadow of her former self. Apart from the loss of one of her funnels and her mainmast her external appearance was hardly changed but inside she was a completely different ship, the renovation work having been limited, in the circumstances, to the minimum necessary to restore her to operational work. She would never again cross the Atlantic as a fully-fledged front-line Cunard ship.

Of the 17 ships of Cunard White Star's prewar passenger fleet, only nine had survived for return to the company to resume commercial sailings: *Queen Elizabeth*, *Queen Mary*, *Aquitania*, now 32 years old and unworthy of a comprehensive overhaul, *Mauretania*, *Britannic*, *Franconia*, *Scythia*, *Samaria* and *Ascania*. It would be some months to come before Cunard could embark on the re-establishment of its scheduled services as the majority of these ships were retained for repatriation work, the last not being released from Government service until the early 1950s.

The Base Repair Ship HMS *Artifex* ex-*Aurania* at Plymouth on 18 May 1944. As the *Aurania*, she had collided with an iceberg in July 1941 while sailing in convoy from Iceland to Halifax. She reached port safely and later survived a torpedo attack.
Imperial War Museum – A 23559

The *Samaria* as a troopship.
Imperial War Museum – CHX 17071

The *Queen Elizabeth* seen arriving in the River Clyde in readiness to take 15,000 GIs on board for return to the United States.
Ian Allan Library

FRANCONIA
1·3·48

▲ The *Mauretania* at the end of the war, with a full complement of repatriated troops. *Imperial War Museum – H 42406*

▼ The *Britannic* at Valletta, Malta on 3 July 1946, her Government auxiliary work still continuing. *Michael Cassar*

◄ On 1 March 1948, almost two years after the end of the war, the *Franconia* calls at Malta while still engaged on repatriation duties, an indication of the huge numbers of persons displaced around the globe by the world conflict. She had nearly suffered the same fate as the *Lancastria* when German aircraft attacked her off Brittany on 16 June 1940. *Michael Cassar*

The *Queen Elizabeth* in the process of conversion back into a liner, moored in the Firth of Clyde at the Tail O' the Bank on 31 May 1946. *Ian Allan Library*

Cunard found itself, after World War 2, facing a similar situation to that which had confronted it following World War 1. The fortunes of war had left its competitors significantly worse off, presenting Cunard with the opportunity to again secure a dominant position on the North Atlantic express run virtually unchallenged. Norddeutscher Lloyd had lost both its giant record-breaking liners. The *Bremen* was destroyed by a fire in March 1941 and her sister *Europa* was seized by the Allies, first for use for troop repatriation and subsequently allocated to the French Line to replace the beautiful *Normandie*, also burnt out in a fire in New York early in 1942. Renamed *Liberté*, the former *Europa* would not re-enter service on the French Line's account until 1950 after a protracted overhaul and reconstruction.

The Italians too had lost both the *Rex* and *Conte di Savoia*, casualties of the fighting, and at that time, the United

States Lines, the principal American competitor, had only the *America* available for the North Atlantic run which ranked with the *Mauretania* rather than with the giant express ships.

The only drawback as far as Cunard was concerned was clearing its residual Government commitments, many of its ships engaged in returning United States and Commonwealth troops and ferrying GI brides across the Atlantic until the late 1940s. Immediately after the war, of course, there were not yet huge numbers of people ready to travel, either for business or pleasure. There followed an interlude in which there was a gradual return to a state of normality, settling the widespread social upheaval and making good the extensive infrastructural damage which affected transport systems as much as anything else.

Cunard used this period as an opportunity to restore its ships and services before demand fully picked up, setting operating policies to reflect the new conditions. The war had introduced or accelerated changes that were to have a direct bearing on the passenger shipping business of the future either immediately or in the longer term.

The expectations of ordinary, working-class people had changed irreversibly and given the opportunity, more now desired to travel and see the world in better circumstances than their wartime experiences had afforded. Colonies and Dominions which had contributed to the Allied cause sought self-determination and the nature of the passenger business to these countries would also change. Many native Britons used the return of peace as an opportunity to relaunch their lives, liberating themselves from the 'Old World' of strife-torn Europe to start anew in the youthful nations of the Commonwealth. And besides these considerations, technology had moved forward with enormous momentum during the war, principally in the field of aviation. With the return of peace, scheduled air services were reintroduced and expanded with a vigour that suggested they would not be in second place to shipping services for very long.

Both Cunard and the new Labour Government considered that prestige dictated top priority for an early restoration of the British presence on the North Atlantic run. In essence, this meant first priority for the release of the *Queen Elizabeth* from Government service as the first Cunard ship to receive her full postwar refit, carried out at her builder's yard on the Clyde and finished at Southampton. She made her maiden commercial sailing from the Hampshire port on 16 October 1946. She looked fresh and resplendent in her Cunard colours against the backdrop of the still drab, bomb-damaged docks and city. At the time, food rationing was still in force for the majority of the population, affecting just about every form of commodity. Thus, it was a joy for those fortunate enough or privileged enough to make that first postwar crossing, to be able to indulge themselves in the mouth-watering range of culinary delights offered during the voyage.

At 83,673 gross tons, the *Queen Elizabeth* was the largest passenger liner in the world, indeed ever built. She

retained this record long after her demise and even though some of the modern cruise ships are now bigger, they only exceed her size in terms of tonnage. The fact was that she actually looked the biggest ship, magnificent and imposing and, like her sister ship *Queen Mary*, her interiors matched the splendour of her outward appearance. She had beautiful, spacious public rooms that oozed quality and style. They were modern, both in design and in choice of materials, but they also retained a certain character that suggested an earlier era when the standards of shipboard décor combined grandeur with tastefulness. None of her successors would display this delicate balance, the design of their public rooms, by comparison, appearing excessive and gaudy.

▲ A later view, on 23 August 1946, as work on her continues at Southampton, looking along the *Queen Elizabeth's* upper decks. *Ian Allan Library*

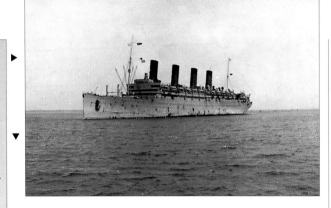

Having made way for her younger consort, the *Queen Mary's* return to service followed just under a year later. She had completed her last troop-carrying voyage on 24 September 1946 and was then sent to the John Brown shipyard for a thorough overhaul and conversion back into a passenger liner.

Her first peacetime departure from Southampton was on 31 July 1947 taking her via Cherbourg and Plymouth to New York. At last Cunard was able to deliver the weekly Atlantic express service it had aspired to launch more than six years earlier. It would not last for as long as might have been hoped but while it was operating it elevated transatlantic travel to a peak of perfection, the like of which will never be experienced again.

To support this unrivalled service, the Port of Southampton commissioned a new passenger terminus building alongside the Ocean Dock. The Ocean Terminal, as it was named, was opened by Prime Minister Clement Attlee on 31 July 1950.

The 'Queens' settled down in their service, popular and well patronised, maintaining the run for almost two decades unbroken. They were both fitted with stabilizers to add to passenger comfort, the *Queen Elizabeth* in 1955 and the *Queen Mary* three years later. One sour note in these days of unsurpassed glory was the emergence of the new American superliner *United States* which wrested the Blue Riband of the Atlantic from the *Queen Mary* on her maiden voyage in July 1952. Just as when the *Mauretania* had been pipped by the *Bremen,* the *Queen Mary* had been vanquished by a ship of a new generation whose margin of improvement had been truly astonishing. No attempt was made to regain the prize by either 'Queen' but a friendly rivalry existed between the three giants from that time on, much as it had done with the *Normandie* before 1939.

Returning to the late 1940s, the old *Aquitania* had continued with troop repatriation work until 1948. It was recognised that she had no future as an Atlantic liner, but there was nevertheless a lot of usefulness left in her. After her release by the British Government she was immediately chartered by the Canadian administration for a series of 12 voyages carrying sponsored passengers from Southampton to Halifax. The accommodation was described euphemistically as 'austere', for the venerable *Aquitania* had not been given any sort of overhaul or refit, the first sailing taking place as early as May 1948. No doubt her emigrant passengers were happy enough, heading off optimistically to their new future in Canada, to tolerate accommodation which was distinctly sub-standard for a ship of the *Aquitania's* pedigree.

The final departure from Halifax for Southampton took

The refurbished *Mauretania*, an aerial view.
David L. Williams Collection

The *Mauretania* enters the King George V Drydock on 14 April 1950 after a programme of cruises to the West Indies.
Ian Allan Library

small provision for passengers. First to appear of this type were the *Media* and *Parthia*, a pair of sleek twin-screw 12,000-tonners. The *Media* was launched on 12 December 1946 and the *Parthia* on 25 February 1947. They operated an Intermediate service from Liverpool to Boston and New York carrying only 250 first-class passengers. The *Media* commenced her maiden voyage on 20 August 1947, the *Parthia* joining her in the following spring, on 10 April 1948. Both had geared steam turbines. Simultaneously, Cunard introduced a number of cargo ships with even more restricted passenger accommodation, in each case offering cabin space for just 12 first-class passengers.

The *Mauretania* had recommenced scheduled operations in the spring of 1947 after a full overhaul and refurbishment at her builder's yard at Birkenhead. Her first postwar sailing began on 26 April 1947 taking her from Liverpool to New York. Thereafter she transferred her home port to Southampton, acting as the relief ship for the *Queen Elizabeth* and *Queen Mary*. Before the war she had supplemented the *Britannic* and *Georgic* on the route from London but this had been terminated, besides which the *Georgic* was no longer in a fit state to resume full passenger-carrying duties.

The *Georgic* had continued as a Government-owned ship managed by Cunard. She remained on troop-carrying work until 1948, being dubbed the 'Super Trooper'. Then, chartered to P&O for the emigrant service to Australia, she was specially refitted for this role by Palmer & Co at Hebburn on the River Tyne, emerging from the shipyard fully restored to her White Star colour scheme. The *Britannic* too perpetuated the old White Star livery after she had undergone a major refit at Belfast in 1947, following the end of her tour of Government duty. This small but welcome gesture was what one would call in modern parlance 'a nice touch', particularly as, from December 1949, White Star ceased altogether to exist as a business entity. As part of a streamlining initiative, the Cunard Steamship Co took over all the assets and liabilities of Cunard White Star, restyling itself as Cunard Line alone from 1 January 1950. But not only did the *Britannic* and *Georgic* retain their original colours – in fact they did so for

▲ place in November 1949 and after her arrival the *Aquitania* was sold off for scrapping at Gare Loch in February 1950, ending one of the most enduring careers of any transatlantic liner. In her 36 years she had steamed over ▶▶ three million miles and had carried 1.2 million passengers. She had made 475 scheduled voyages across the Atlantic, or 580 in total if her wartime crossings and emigrant passages are included. She was not replaced.

Cunard did not launch a major rebuilding programme after World War 2 as it had done in the 1920s. Having the two 'Queens', there was no need to commission new large passenger vessels. As for the other, lesser services it set about the restoration of the surviving tonnage. Those new vessels that were ordered were for the most part all small in size, with a large cargo-carrying capacity and only a very the remainder of their lives – they also continued to fly the White Star houseflag superior to the lion rampant of Cunard. Interestingly, between 1935 and 1949, Cunard vessels had flown the two flags the other way round.

Her refit complete, the *Britannic* established a new Liverpool to New York service carrying 429 first-class passengers and 564 in tourist-class. Her début sailing was on 22 May 1948. She maintained this route well into the 1950s, occasionally partnered by her former sister, until late in her life she was switched to full-time cruising.

Meanwhile, the *Georgic* continued with her sailings to Australia out of Liverpool, on one voyage carrying a record 2,010 emigrants. She also brought Jamaican immigrants to the United Kingdom. Cunard occasionally chartered her for North Atlantic work from 1950 but she was far from ideal with her low-grade, one-class accommodation. Her end came in 1955 after a final phase of work chartered to the Australian Government. She arrived at her home port of Liverpool for the last time on 19 November 1955. Two months later she bade her final farewell, destined for Faslane and breaking up.

Only one large new ship featured in the Cunard building programme after World War 2, the yacht-like dual-role *Caronia*, launched on 30 October 1947 by Princess Elizabeth, the future Queen. The *Caronia* broke many Cunard traditions. She was the first ship specially built with extensive cruising in mind, the intention being for her to supplement the *Mauretania's* New York sailings from Southampton for part of the year. With her unique role in mind, she introduced a totally new colour scheme, painted in three shades of green. Her raked lines were surmounted by a single squat funnel – surely one of the largest ever built on a ship – mounted behind a single tripod mast, placed above her bridge.

As the years progressed into the late 1950s cruising became an increasingly important dimension of Cunard's operations, an activity which the *Caronia* largely dominated. Long before that, though, the Canadian services were also the focus of restoration effort, benefiting from the only class of new liners constructed for Cunard over a period of 22 years.

The *Mauretania* resumed commercial sailings in April 1947. She is seen here berthed at New York.
Ian Shiffmann

The *Queen Mary* arriving at Southampton. *Ian Shiffmann*

The elegant single-class cargo-passenger ship *Parthia*. *Ian Allan Library* ▶

The *Queen Mary* in the Ocean Dock. With the *Queen Elizabeth* she dominated the Atlantic passenger trade until its decline in the 1960s. *David L. Williams Collection* ◀

Arriving at New York, the *Queen Mary* completes another transatlantic voyage. *Ian Allan Library* ▼

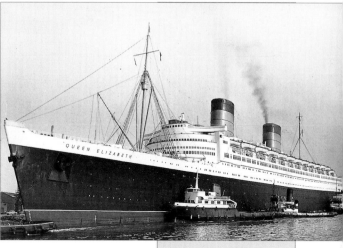

▲ Seen again at Southampton, a splendid view of the *Queen Elizabeth* with the tugs *Gatcombe*, *Clausentum* and *Romsey*.
Roger Sherlock Collection

▼ The *Queen Mary* entering the King George V Drydock, Southampton on 16 July 1948. *British Transport Docks Board*

◄ The *Queen Elizabeth* and the Ocean Terminal, Southampton, both intrinsically linked with the transatlantic Ferry.
David L. Williams Collection

▲

Aerial view of the *Queen Mary* in the Ocean Dock, Southampton, at the time of the 1966 seamen's strike. *Ian Shiffmann*

Alongside at Liverpool, the motor-liner *Britannic* survived as the last vestige of the old White Star fleet until December 1960. *Ian Shiffmann*

The *Britannic*, here in a
trials photograph, looked
much the same for the
remainder of her career,
whereas the *Georgic*, which
was retained only for
emigrant-carrying work,
was altered considerably.
Ian Allan Library

The cargo-passenger liner
Media. Alex Duncan

The *Georgic* postwar,
employed on the
transportation of settlers to
the southern Dominions.
Ian Allan Library

7. THE DOMINION SERVICES – THE FINAL DECADES

Reinstatement of the Cunard Line services to Canada after World War 2 depended initially on the return to the passenger trade of the *Franconia, Samaria* and *Scythia*, the three surviving ships from the prewar Intermediate class.

As the new *Media* and *Parthia* had been placed on the Intermediate run to New York, Cunard no longer required the three older vessels for this work. When they were released from wartime auxiliary duties, they were employed instead as a stop-gap measure on the Dominion route pending the availability of new ships.

All three had enjoyed long and distinguished wartime careers extending to late in the 1940s. In February 1945 the *Franconia* had the honour of being selected as the headquarters ship for the Allied Conference at Yalta, in the Crimea, between Prime Minister Winston Churchill, the United States President Franklin D. Roosevelt and President of the Soviet Union, Josef Stalin.

Between 1945 and 1948, the *Franconia, Scythia* and *Samaria* were engaged returning Canadian servicemen and their families from Europe, also in the carriage of displaced persons to Canada in voyages organised by the International Refugee Organisation. In this period they retained their grey auxiliary hulls, but their funnels were repainted in Cunard colours.

First to be released from Government service was the *Franconia* which underwent an overhaul and refit prior to returning to the Liverpool to Quebec and Montreal service, making her first sailing on 2 June 1949. Her accommodation areas had been restyled to cater for 250 first-class and 600 tourist-class passengers. After extensive reconditioning, the *Scythia* and *Samaria* were also placed on the Dominion run. Initially, from 17 August 1950, the *Scythia* sailed from Liverpool but from 10 April 1951 she switched to Southampton. The *Samaria*, on the other hand, worked out of Southampton from her very first postwar crossing. Accommodation layout on the latter pair was broadly the same as on the *Franconia* with slightly more tourist-class berths.

The *Samaria* was selected to represent the Cunard line at the Coronation Naval Review at Spithead on 15 June 1953. She was joined for the occasion by the *Strathnaver* of P&O Line, the *Orcades* from Orient Line, Union Castle Line's *Pretoria Castle* and the *Andes*, the flagship of Royal Mail Line, besides countless other naval and mercantile ships, a huge armada totalling more than 300. Across from her in 'D' line,

◄ The *Franconia* was switched to the Canadian Dominion service after World War 2. *Ian Allan Library*

▼ Last surviving unit of the prewar, six-ship 'A' class, the *Ascania* in the early 1950s. *Ian Allan Library*

The *Carinthia* in the Mersey River.
Ian Shiffmann

Lead ship of the new Dominion service quartet, the magnificent
Saxonia at speed on 11 September 1954.
Ian Allan Library

▲ barely a half-mile away was her former fleetmate *Alaunia*.

For a period these three liners were supported on the Canadian services by the refurbished *Ascania*, the only unit of the old 'A' class to be returned to Cunard after the war. The other surviving ships of this group had been retained by the Admiralty to see out their days as naval repair ships stationed at Devonport, Chatham and Rosyth.

The *Ascania* had opened an austerity service from Liverpool to Halifax, beginning on 20 December 1947, carrying emigrants to Canada. Just over a year later she was taken in hand for overhaul and reconditioning after which she returned to the Liverpool to Quebec and Montreal service working alongside the *Franconia*. As refitted, her accommodation provided for 200 passengers in first-class and 500 in tourist-class. She survived until December 1956 when she was disposed of for scrapping at Newport, South Wales, displaced by the incoming quartet of newly-built liners.

Planning for the replacement of the *Franconia, Scythia, Samaria* and *Ascania* had commenced in the early 1950s with shipyard contracts awarded from 1953. All four were placed with John Brown, Clydebank. The fact that this was the only full class of new ships constructed for Cunard after World War 2 was more than compensated for by their quality and stylishness. They were striking-looking ships, nicely raked with a good turn of speed and they seemed to stand out in their Cunard colours more than any others with, perhaps, the exception of the 'Queens'.

Two were built for the Canadian services from Southampton, the *Saxonia*, first of the class, and *Ivernia,* and two for the route from Liverpool, the *Carinthia* and *Sylvania*, although the four ships occasionally alternated, as dictated by operational needs. They were the largest Cunard ships ever to be designed and built specially for the Canadian routes. Measuring approximately 22,000 gross tons each, they were powered by geared steam turbines driving twin screws, giving a service speed of 20kt, permitting them to reduce the previous best passage times by two days. Their accommodation for 125 first-class and 800 in tourist-class exhibited a quality and standard hitherto unseen on this run. The public rooms were spacious, modern and beautifully decorated. Maple and sycamore, types of wood associated with Canada, were widely used in the panelling and other features. Similarly the frontier spirit of Canada was emphasised through the many images and pictures which evoked the individual characters of each province. Their accommodation could be combined to form a single class when they were sent cruising.

The *Saxonia* was launched on 17 February 1954 by Lady Churchill and entered service on 2 September 1954, her first voyage leaving from Liverpool. On 1 July 1955 she was joined by the *Ivernia* which had been launched on 14 December of the previous year.

Third of the class, the *Carinthia* was launched by Princess Margaret on 14 December 1955. Her maiden voyage began on 27 June 1956. Completing the quartet, the *Sylvania* made her début on 5 June 1957. By this time, three of the vessels they had replaced had been sold for breaking up, the *Samaria* at Inverkeithing in January 1956, the already mentioned *Ascania* and the *Franconia* which ended her life at Rosyth in December 1956. Last to be disposed of was the *Scythia* which was scrapped at Inverkeithing from 1958 after a brief period providing cover while the new ships got into their stride.

In 1957, the four 'Saxonia' class ships had Denny Brown stabilizers installed to improve passenger comfort, part of an almost fleet-wide programme of improvements which saw the 'Queens', the *Mauretania* and *Caronia* fitted with the same equipment. Other improvements included the provision of air conditioning on the *Mauretania* and *Caronia*.

Befitting its status as the market leader, Cunard could again boast a superb fleet of 10 of the best ships on the North Atlantic run: the *Queen Mary* and *Queen Elizabeth* were the largest and, without question, the most luxurious of the ships serving New York; the cargo-passenger vessels *Media* and *Parthia* offered an exclusive, high grade of passage on the Intermediate service to the United States and, in the *Mauretania* and *Caronia*, Cunard had a second-rank liner and a unique dual-role ship which both surpassed the first-rank ships of many other lines. Now it had in operation the four biggest and best ships it had ever placed on the Canadian services. Only Canadian Pacific's 'Empress' liners exceeded them in size.

But commercial fortunes being what they are, in an ever changing world, Cunard was fated to bask in the glory of its fresh achievements for only a very few years...

▲ The *Ivernia*.
World Ship Photo Library

▼ The *Franconia's* sister ship, the *Scythia* seen in March 1951. The third surviving sister, the *Samaria*, represented the Cunard Line at the Coronation Fleet Review off Spithead in 1953.
Maritime Photo Library

The *Carinthia*. *Ian Shiffmann* ▲

In the River Mersey in
1963, the *Carinthia*. ▶
Maritime Photo Library

The *Queen Elizabeth* in the ▶▶
early 1960s.
David L. Williams Collection

8.   SERIOUS CRUISING

▶ After World War 2, Cunard somewhat modified its cruising
policy compared with that of the prewar years, setting an
operational pattern that continued until the end of the
1950s. While the majority of the passenger vessels were
included in a programme of off-peak cruising, gone was
the use of cruise work as a temporary expedient to offset
low levels of utilisation. Line voyage work was to remain
the main source of income for the foreseeable future. For
the first time, Cunard added a purpose-designed cruising
ship to its fleet, the dual-role *Caronia*. For part of the
season she would provide back-up on the North Atlantic
route but for the rest of the year she would be dedicated to
long-distance, dollar-earning luxury cruises, unashamedly
directed at a clientèle who were largely in the millionaire
bracket.

Befitting her unique role, she was given an equally
distinctive colour scheme of three shades of green.
Psychologists will tell you that green is the most relaxing
colour in the spectrum, but whether this paint scheme was
selected through such deep analysis of human reaction to
sensory stimuli or was simply the result of more superficial
reasoning is not known, but it was not long before the
Caronia was nicknamed the 'Green Goddess'.

Ordered in 1946, she was launched on 30 October 1947
by Princess Elizabeth, the future Queen, as a further
testimony that Britain was slowly but surely emerging
from the dull plainness of the austere postwar era. The
Caronia opened her account with a maiden sailing from
Southampton to New York on 4 January 1949. Thereafter,
she established a year-round routine alternating between
excursions and route voyages, something of a fair-weather
ship in that wherever her travels took her it was invariably
the best time of year.

 Her furnishings and decorations were truly magnificent
as might be expected of a ship designed to attract the most
discerning of travellers. And she was extraordinarily
popular. Some of her wealthier customers booked

accommodation on her and stayed aboard for such long periods that she almost became a floating hotel, if not their home at sea.

Throughout the 1950s, Cunard continued to offer sea tours along these lines, the shorter off-season cruises being supported by almost all the other ships of the fleet, their rigid accommodation layouts not really suiting longer cruise trips.

However, as the years advanced and the transition to airline travel across the Atlantic increased, Cunard was compelled, as it had been in the 1930s, although for quite different reasons, to switch more of its ships to cruising and for longer periods. The whole problem was exaggeratedly caricatured in a cartoon in one of the travel trade publications of the time. The scene depicted two

▲ Immediately after the launch, the *Caronia* about to be towed to the fitting-out berth. *Ian Allan Library*

◄ Fitting out at Clydebank, the almost complete *Caronia* on 17 November 1948. *Ian Allan Library*

The *Caronia*, a stylish postcard impression of Cunard's novel cruise ship. *Philip Rentell Collection*

▲ travel shops in a typical High Street, one vibrantly busy selling airline tickets, its customers queuing outside onto the pavement, the other, specialising in steamship travel, empty and quiet. Inside the latter, two assistants are seated at the reception counter, one leaning back in a chair, stifling a yawn, the other playing what purports to be an endless game of Patience. Above them and to their side on the wall is a small glass-fronted cabinet containing a solitary ticket in the name of a contrived ocean liner company. Beneath it, the legend reads: 'In case of passenger, break glass.'

Clearly things were not quite that extreme, but Cunard was compelled, nevertheless, to increase the time its ships were sent on cruises in preference to making half-full, or more pertinently, half-empty, scheduled voyages. It is true to say that there were times when, given the labour-intensive hotel side of passenger ship operations, the two 'Queen' liners carried more crew than fare-paying passengers.

So it was that the nature of employment of the Cunard passenger ships progressively changed. In 1958 the

Mauretania was fully air-conditioned and used for year-round world cruising. Since her return to passenger service in 1947 she had made cruises out of New York in the winter months but from this time on she would be used for little else. The old *Britannic* too was almost exclusively devoted to cruising from New York until, in November 1960, she made a final Liverpool to New York crossing prior to disposal for demolition.

The *Queen Elizabeth* and *Queen Mary* were also engaged more extensively in making cruises, with a corresponding reduction in the number of line voyages on offer each year. Their tours to the Caribbean, though arranged with rather more serious considerations in mind, were reminiscent of some of the spectacular prewar cruises made by the giant liners, notably the *Normandie's* excursion to Brazil in 1938.

In 1962, the *Mauretania* was taken in hand for further modifications befitting her extended cruise role. These included the construction of a lido deck. When she left the shipyard that December, at the end of the work, she also had been painted in the green colouring scheme introduced with the *Caronia*. Repositioned in the Mediterranean, she was predominantly employed cruising in that area, making, in addition, occasional Atlantic crossings on a Naples to New York service.

From the early 1960s, the ships working the St Lawrence route also began to feel the pinch, necessitating quite drastic adjustments to timetables and vessel deployments in the face of ever-declining revenues and profitability.

In 1962 the *Saxonia* and *Ivernia* were more or less totally withdrawn from the Dominion service for conversion into full-time cruise ships, although, like the *Caronia*, they were euphemistically promoted as dual-role vessels. Both had been engaged on a growing programme of winter cruises based at Port Everglades but the changes planned for them would make for a more complete metamorphosis. Like the *Mauretania*, they had lido decks built into the structure abaft their funnels, displacing the derricks originally installed there. They also received the coat of green paint which by now was accepted as the symbolic outward manifestation of a Cunard ship whose primary

◀ The millionaire-class cruises of the *Caronia* took her to the four corners of the globe. Here she is at Wellington, New Zealand. *Ian Shiffmann*

▼ As cruise activity increased, the *Saxonia* became the *Carmania*. Her hull and upperworks were painted white in keeping with her new role. *Ian Shiffmann*

The spectacular *Caronia* enters service. She had one of the largest funnels ever built on to a ship. Indeed, it was so big that, apparently, it affected the manoeuvrability of the ship at slow speeds if there was a strong wind blowing.
Ian Allan Library

The *Franconia* at Southampton in June 1963.
Maritime Photo Library

function was to be cruising. The *Saxonia* was renamed *Carmania*, the *Ivernia*, in turn, receiving the new name *Franconia*.

For the next six or so years, from early 1963, they were used on Mediterranean fly-cruises, taking advantage of the very form of transport that had undermined their traditional livelihoods as aircraft were used to ferry passengers to the ports of embarkation. Occasional voyages *were* made to Canada, from Rotterdam and Southampton, but these steadily reduced in number.

The other pair from the Dominion services' quartet continued, for the time being at least, on the run to Canada from Liverpool, as far as possible providing business as usual. Ultimately, though, the creeping cancer afflicting the scheduled ocean passenger liner business reached them, too. In 1967 they were given white hulls, in something of a break from the trend that Cunard had established, and they also found themselves diverted to cruise voyages.

Between October and December 1965, the *Caronia* underwent a major refit, in the course of which her passenger accommodation was thoroughly modernised. Befitting her specialist role, a lido deck was fitted aft and two large launches, for ferrying tour passengers ashore, were installed on either side of her foredeck, immediately in front of the bridge. This was a practice later copied on the cruise ship *Norway* after she had been purpose-converted from the transatlantic liner *France*.

To the best of its ability, Cunard had adapted its fleet operations in the face of adversity to maintain and sustain a viable shipping business but the pace of events was quickening rapidly and the writing was on the wall. The aircraft which had 'stolen' the point-to-point travel business from the ocean liners would not go away and in this context, switching ships to cruising as if to deal with a temporary 'blip' was totally inappropriate. If ocean passenger ships were to survive it would be as pure cruise vessels, in a sense floating resorts, designed and built specially for this role and not modified within an old shell, like a plastic veneer hiding rotten wood.

Cunard, like many other shipping companies, came to

Montreal Harbour with either the *Carmania* or *Franconia* in the foreground. *Ian Allan Library*

The *Franconia* ex-*Ivernia* in cruise livery berthed at New York.
Ian Shiffmann

The *Queen Elizabeth* off Cowes, Isle of Wight, on a bright, summer's day in the mid-1960s. At that time, with circumstances dictating that she undertook cruises to increase her earnings, she was just as likely to be seen moored off a Caribbean island.
David L. Williams Collection

appreciate this, recognising that, apart from their fundamental unsuitability for serious cruise work, conceived initially with quite different objectives in mind, the older converted vessels were much more expensive to maintain and run. In effect, further renovation would amount to throwing good money after bad.

It was a turning point. Many of the established shipping companies would not make the transition and would disappear from the sealanes forever. Cunard, true to its glorious traditions, would survive and grow, but first many of the old units of the fleet would have to go.

The *Mauretania* finally went for breaking up at Inverkeithing in November 1965. The *Caronia,* popular when cruising but not so on the transatlantic service was,

The green-hulled
Mauretania.
Tom Rayner Collection

The *Mauretania* with the
Queen Mary in the Ocean
Dock, Southampton.
Southern Daily Echo

in the end, a dual-role experiment that had been only partially successful. Despite the fact that her accommodation had been fully modernised in October 1965, she made her final Cunard voyage late in 1967 and was then transferred between a number of dubious foreign shipping concerns, ostensibly for continued cruise operation. After extensive periods of lay-up and the occasional venture to sea which was nothing short of a fiasco, she was sent for breaking up in 1974. Under the new name *Caribia*, given to her back in 1968, she avoided the ignominy of the cutter's torch, impaling herself on rocks at Apra on the island of Guam after breaking free from her towline. Here the sea finished her off, her once resplendent green hull broken into three sections, reducing her to a total wreck.

As for the *Carinthia* and *Sylvania*, they were laid up at Southampton in 1968, abandoned barely a year after the start of their new operation. They languished for over two years until purchased by the Italian state-owned shipping company, Sitmar, again ostensibly for further conversion for route work between Italy and Australia, one of the few remaining opportunities for this kind of service. In the event, the line traffic to Australia never materialised and they were switched to full-time cruising.

The *Carmania* and *Franconia* lasted a little longer, assisting Cunard as it migrated into a whole new era of ocean passenger business.

◄ The *Caronia* assisted by the tug *Gladstone*. *Roger Sherlock Collection*

▲ The *Sylvania* in white cruising livery. The word 'CUNARD' would later be painted on either side of her hull. *World Ship Photo Library*

▼ Another port, another cruise – the *Caronia* in Valletta Harbour, Malta. *David L. Williams Collection*

CUNARD QUALITY CRUiSES

ATLANTIC ISLES
WEST INDIES
MEDITERRANEAN

BIG SHIP CRUISING
AT ITS BEST

QUEEN MARY
MAURETANIA

◄◄ In 1962, the *Mauretania* was converted for cruise work and to run a transatlantic service from the Mediterranean, from a new base at Naples. Here she is in her new colours. *Ian Shiffmann*

◄◄ The *Sylvania* in white cruising colours. *Ian Shiffmann*

◄ 'Big Ship Cruising at its Best', Cunard advertisement for the *Queen Mary* and *Mauretania*. *Ian Allan Library*

9. GLORY IN TRANSITION

▲ By 1960, the *Queen Mary* and *Queen Elizabeth* were 24 and 20 years old respectively and thought had to be given to their replacement in the not too distant future. These were uncertain times for the passenger shipping industry and there were influential forces within it who debated, not how the two great liners should be replaced, but whether they should be replaced at all. Besides this, undertakings on the scale of building new superliners were enormously expensive, well beyond the company's own means. Inevitably, Government money would be needed to help finance the project. With this in mind, the Government set up a committee under Lord Chandos to review the options and make recommendations on the best course of action.

Meanwhile, sensing the imminence of a prestigious order for what the shipping press had already dubbed the '*Q3*', shipyards were developing designs for the new ship, taking into consideration Cunard's determination to maintain the supremacy on the Atlantic that it had enjoyed since 1945. Although the United States Lines remained a significant presence on the North Atlantic, having the newest vessel on the run, still the speed record holder, the French Line nevertheless represented the more serious competition from Cunard's point of view. The French Line had its own problems with regard to how it should deal with the imminent retirement of the *Liberté* and *Ile de France,* both of which were older than the 'Queens'. In the event they opted for a traditional style of vessel, at least in the sense of its intended function, seemingly ending the speculation over the intention to maintain the regular passenger trade across the Atlantic. And the new liner, the *France*, was no half-measure; she projected not the slightest hint in her style, dimensions or appointments that she was other than a classic giant intended exclusively for this type of work. The *France* was elegant for such a large vessel, in some ways a reminder of the beautiful prewar *Normandie*. She was the longest passenger liner ever built and, at the time, the third largest, surpassed only by the *Queen Mary* and *Queen Elizabeth*.

All this served to reinforce the view that Cunard's replacement ships would follow the same pattern; there was even a certain anxiety that Cunard should not delay for too long making its own commitment in the face of this new rivalry. Design concepts for the *Q3* were firmed up, revealing an equally large vessel of around 75,000 gross tons though somewhat shorter than the *France* at just under 1,000ft in length. The ship's hull was fairly conventional, exhibiting a modern rake with partially turtle-backed foredeck. The funnel designs were in a state of flux, the aft most, evolving from one that was large, broad-based and curved, very much in keeping with contemporary fashions, into a slim flute of an exhaust similar to that on the later *Queen Elizabeth 2*. A second, forward funnel was blended into the foremast, to some extent disguising its purpose.

Like the earlier 'Queens', the *Q3* would have been a quadruple-screw, steam turbine ship capable of a service speed of 28kt to meet the requirements of the weekly sailing timetable. Interestingly, provision was made for future adaptation from oil to nuclear fuel for her boilers.

The Chandos Committee eventually came out in favour of this type of ship, but while recommending that the Government should extend a loan to Cunard on preferential terms, this was to enable it to build only one such new vessel, not two. There was talk for a while of encouraging Cunard to merge with P&O or at least seek a closer affiliation as part of such a deal, though it is hard to see what possible benefits would have been gained from such a move. These concerns were not competing against each other, operating, as they did, on quite different route networks.

Col Denis Bates, the Cunard Chairman, had died in September 1959 at the age of 73. He was an unashamed champion of the 'Big Ship' policy, resolute in his conviction that Cunard should continue to operate ships of this class as the dominant force in North Atlantic shipping. His successor, Sir John Brocklebank, was not of the same persuasion, favouring a smaller replacement vessel suited for adaptation to satisfy the changing needs of the industry. In the light of poor trading results in 1961, he elected to postpone a decision on the *Q3* while the board studied the design further and considered all the alternative options. Some might call it prevarication, the indecision lasting for over three years, but in retrospect it was a wise course of action, although realistically it spelt the end for the *Q3* concept there and then. The truth was that, behind closed doors, the *Q3* had been regarded as a recipe for disaster.

In fact, 1961 was not the only bad year for Cunard. The company had been losing money steadily for some considerable time, some £14 million in total (today the equivalent of more than £160 million) since 1955. By 1964, despite there being no improvement to the trading situation,

Sir John Brocklebank gave a clearer indication of the type of substitute ship the company preferred to commission, promising that the contract for the new vessel would be awarded before the end of that December. Despite the dubious experience with the Caronia, a part-time cruise liner, part-time route voyage ship, the 'Q4', as the replacement ship was now identified, was envisaged as a dual-role vessel, but more as a top-grade mobile hotel than an ocean liner. The intention was that in the summer season she would ply the Atlantic and for the rest of the year, essentially during the winter months, she would become a sun-seeking resort, creaming off the leisure traffic.

Certainly, the concept appeared to be more practical for, with ever declining passenger numbers on scheduled

▲ The *Queen Mary* at 107 berth, New Docks, Southampton on the night of 30 October 1967, the day before her final departure. *Ian Allan Library*

Artist's impression of the 'Q3' design, the original concept for the replacements for the older 'Queens', in effect a modern version of the conventional regular service liner.
Edward Bearman

The *Queen Mary's* last sailing from New York, bound for Long Beach and a future of preservation as the most enduring monument of the age of the passenger liner.
Ian Shiffmann

CUNARD
1969
£ Timetable and fares

Revised edition April, 1969

▲ Seen off the Isle of Wight, the *Queen Elizabeth 2* heads for her home port, Southampton. *Barry Elliott*

◄◄ Timetable and fares tariff for the *Queen Elizabeth 2's* first season, published in April 1969, depicting a model of the new flagship. *Cunard Line – Ian Allan Library*

◄ The retired *Queen Elizabeth* at Port Everglades, Florida where she was to have been converted into a hotel ship and convention centre. *David L. Williams Collection*

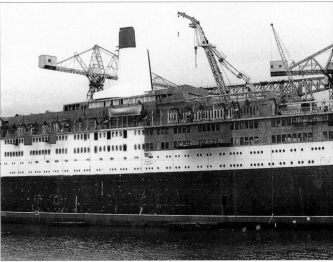

voyages, Cunard could not continue to operate ships like
the 'Queens' at a loss. The fact was that, unlike the *France*
and the *United States*, Cunard's operation was not
subsidised by the Government. In fact, it never had been.
To Cunard's enduring credit, given the scale of service it
had maintained, it had always generated all of its revenue
itself through ticket sales and mail contracts and, for the
larger part of its existence, it had operated profitably.

The order for the *Q4*, the *Queen Elizabeth 2* as she would
be christened, was placed on 30 December 1964. She
would be built in the same John Brown shipyard as her
predecessors.

That same year saw another change of Chairman when
Sir John Brocklebank retired through ill health. The
incoming Chairman was Sir Basil Smallpiece who set
about a comprehensive rescue plan for Cunard which, in
reality, was now seriously ailing, being a shadow of the
once glorious shipping concern of only a few years earlier.
Aided by a team of consultants he launched a thorough
overhaul of the entire business. Simultaneously, the
Economist Intelligence Unit was engaged to carry out an
in-depth study of the travel and cruise markets for ships.

From these exercises, Cunard received much plain-
speaking advice, a number of self-evident truths which
they needed to act upon swiftly.

Essentially, to remain in the passenger shipping
business, the ships had to pay their way or, at the very
minimum, break even. Cruising had to be pursued more
vigorously and more purposefully as an integral part of
Cunard's passenger business portfolio. The medicine was
bitter to swallow but it was taken, every drop.

The essential ingredients of the proposed shake-up were
a fundamental reorganisation of the business, a rational-
isation of the cargo operations, diversification into other
profitable business areas and, as feared, sweeping fleet cuts.

Arising from the recommendations, Cunard totally
relocated its headquarters to Southampton, severing
completely its long links with Liverpool and selling off its
building there. Other economies included the closure of
Cunard's offices in Paris, Le Havre and Dublin. The
company's premises on Broadway, New York and at
Leadenhall Street, London were also sold. Fleet disposals
were drastic, cutting the number of ships from the 10 in
1961 to just three in 1969 and creating 2,700 redundancies

in the process. The *Media* and *Parthia* had already been sold to new operators for continued trading in 1961. The later disposal of the *Mauretania* and *Caronia*, for scrap, has already been described. Now it was the turn of the 'Queens'. The end for the *Queen Mary* and the *Queen Elizabeth*, for all that it had been long anticipated, was nevertheless a sorrowful experience when it finally became a reality.

The *Queen Mary* completed her 1,000th Atlantic crossing in the autumn of 1967. She was then sold to Long Beach Corporation for retention as a static museum exhibit, hotel and convention centre as well as an occasional movie set. She left Southampton for the last time on 31 October 1967. It was a grey, downcast day which reflected the sombre mood of the vast crowds at the docks and lining the shores of the Solent, there to witness her final departure much as more joyful well-wishers had seen her off on her maiden voyage, 31 years before. After paying a final call at New York, the *Queen Mary* became the first and only Cunarder to round Cape Horn for, being too large to pass through the Panama Canal, she was compelled to take this route in order to reach California. After a lengthy restoration, some of it frowned upon by purists, she opened to the public on 10 May 1971. She has experienced mixed fortunes since then, with a number of changes of ownership, but she still survives as an enduring monument to the great days of the Atlantic Ferry.

The *Queen Elizabeth's* passing did not occasion by quite the same degree of pathos as that of her older partner, and neither was her subsequent career blessed with the same degree of good fortune. Her final departure from Southampton on 29 November 1968 took her to Port Everglades, Florida where it was proposed to convert her too into a permanent shipping museum and convention centre. However, her new owners were not as adequately prepared financially for such an undertaking and stripped of 'Queen' in her name she was also gradually stripped of the dignity normally associated with such a title.

Languishing there for two years, the prospects of a more fitting employment to end her days were heralded in 1970 when the Chinese shipping magnate C. Y. Tung purchased

her. His aim was to adapt her into a mobile, international University of the Sea, to foster brotherhood between the youth of all nations. But it was not to be. With the conversion nearing completion, and the ship now bearing the name *Seawise University*, she burnt out in a funeral pyre at Hong Kong on 9 January 1972. It was a kind of Valhalla that seemed, on reflection, to be a far more appropriate end to such a great liner and the era she represented.

Pending the inauguration of the new *Queen Elizabeth 2*, Cunard was left with just four ships: the former Dominion services quartet. For a year or so they had been dedicated to cruise work, painted white with the company name painted prominently on their sides, as if it had become necessary to reaffirm their origins and ownership. Now they were reduced to only two, when the *Sylvania* and *Carinthia* were sold to Italian operators in 1970. These were not the best of times for Cunard, caught between its glorious past and what it hoped would be a more auspicious future.

Along with the other aspects of the root and branch reorganisation of the late 1960s, Cunard adopted a new marketing strategy which it set about promoting

The third 'Queen' liner, the *Queen Elizabeth 2*, complete and in service. Initially there was disappointment because she did not wear Cunard's famous red and black colours on her single, modern funnel.
Cunard Line

The *Seawise University* ex-*Queen Elizabeth* called at Cape Town en route to Hong Kong where she was to be converted into a University ship. *Ian Shiffmann*

◀◀ Ablaze from end to end, the fate of the *Seawise University* is prematurely sealed.
David L. Williams Collection

◀ The *Queen Elizabeth 2's* stylish modern lines were prominently featured in Cunard publicity material promoting the new liner. This poster was by William A. Sloan.
David L. Williams Collection

▼ The *Caribia* ex-*Caronia* listing heavily to port and swept by huge waves. She was soon reduced to a total wreck.
United States Navy

energetically. Considering that the company was not alone in its misfortunes it desired to be among the front-runners when passenger shipping ultimately emerged from its trough. Cunard's view was that passenger ships should no longer be regarded as simply a means of transport but, even when travelling, as floating resorts, places of holiday and relaxation: 'Half the fun is in getting there.' In this way it sought to dissociate itself from the ocean travel market, perceived as contracting and in steep decline, and align itself to the new and fast-expanding leisure industry.

The *Queen Elizabeth 2* was very much a ship of this philosophy, in keeping with the resurgent spirit of the times. For Cunard, she was the crowning glory at the end of the most difficult decade ever experienced. Launched on 20 September 1967 by Her Majesty Queen Elizabeth, she entered service with a series of shakedown cruises commencing on 22 April 1969. Her maiden voyage to New York began 10 days later.

Unlike the earlier 'Queen' liners, the *Queen Elizabeth 2* is a twin-screw ship though still with a designed service speed of 28kt. Beyond her early years no attempt was made to perpetuate a rigorous, regular line schedule with her.

The design of her interiors is modern and stylish, even lavish, while avoiding any attempt to recreate the past. Instead her décor reflects the tastes and needs of a new generation of passengers and cruise-makers. For long, her operating background was turbulent as Cunard gradually migrated into a fully-fledged cruise ship operator.

The old *Franconia* and *Carmania* were sold to the Soviet Union in the early 1970s, being too expensive to maintain and operate at the standard dictated by the highly competitive cruising industry. Their replacements, the *Cunard Adventurer* and *Cunard Ambassador* were the first of a series of purpose-designed cruise ships commissioned by Cunard as it sought to find the right blend of vessels across its entire operation.

The years since have witnessed changes of ownership for Cunard and, for the *Queen Elizabeth 2*, bomb scares, call-up for military service at the time of the Falklands War and, more recently, conversion from steamship to motorship when her main machinery was changed to diesel-electric plant. Undoubtedly, the *Queen Elizabeth 2* has been a resounding success. Cunard worked wonders carving out a

The *Seawise University* ex-*Queen Elizabeth* engulfed by fire at Hong Kong on 9 January 1972. *L. L. von Münching*

The *Caribia*, the once beautiful *Caronia*, in her death throes stranded off Apra, Guam in August 1974. *United States Navy*

niche market for this, the flagship of the British Merchant Marine, her following being the envy of other operators and reminiscent of the patronage attracted by certain units of the 'Big Three' half a century earlier. Her world cruises have become legendary, reaching parts no other cruise ships reach. Today, restyled and restored to Cunard's traditional colours, she looks better than ever.

Now as the 20th century draws to a close, she remains the gem in the Cunard crown, a prestigious vessel servicing the luxury end of the market and a vestigial link to Cunard's great heritage and long traditions. Having already spanned the best part of two centuries, Cunard's glorious presence on the ocean highways, in the *Queen Elizabeth 2* and whatever ships follow her, is sure to continue into a new century and a new millennium.

▲ The modern cruise ship *Cunard Adventurer*, the first such vessel commissioned by Cunard, perpetuated its new colouring scheme and introduced a naming convention which was another departure from tradition.
World Ship Photo Library

◄ Twelve years after her entry into service, the *Queen Elizabeth 2* was taken over as a troopship at the time of the Falklands conflict. Here she is returning to Southampton at the end of her tour of duty.
Peter A. Alford

The *Cunard Adventurer* after her funnel was repainted in the traditional Cunard black and red colours.
Ian Shiffmann

On a sunlit evening, the *Queen Elizabeth 2* is seen at New York wearing the traditional Cunard colours in her last days as a steamship. After a difficult start to her career, the *Queen Elizabeth 2* proved ultimately to be a winner, building up a dedicated following and an impressive reputation. For Cunard, the enduring question remains: how, when the time comes, is it to replace a vessel of this calibre?
Moran Towing & Transportation

Caronia (1905-32)
John Brown, Clydebank, launched 13 July 1904.
19,687grt; 678ft loa.
Passengers: (as built) 300 first-class, 350 second-class, 900 third-class, 1,100 steerage; (from 1924) 425 cabin-class, 365 tourist-class, 650 third-class.
Crew: 700.
Engines: quadruple expansion steam reciprocating, 22,000ihp; twin screw, 18kt.
Fate: broken up in Japan, March 1933, under name *Taiseiyo Maru*.

Carmania (1905-32)
John Brown, Clydebank, launched 21 February 1905.
19,566grt; 675ft loa.
Passengers: (as built) 300 first-class, 350 second-class, 900 third-class, 1,100 steerage; (from 1924) 425 cabin-class, 365 tourist-class, 650 third-class.
Crew: 700.
Engines: direct acting steam turbines, 21,000shp; triple screw, 18kt.
Fate: broken up at Blyth, March 1932.

Mauretania (1907-35)
Swan, Hunter & Wigham Richardson, Wallsend, launched 20 September 1906.
31,938grt; 790ft loa.
Passengers: (as built) 563 first-class, 464 second-class, 1,138 third-class; (from 1921) 589 first-class, 400 second-class, 767 third-class.
Crew: 812.
Engines: direct acting steam turbines, 78,000shp; quadruple screw, 25kt.
Fate: broken up at Rosyth, July 1935.

Aquitania (1914-50)
John Brown, Clydebank, launched 21 April 1913.
45,647grt; 901ft loa.
Passengers: (as built) 618 first-class, 614 second-class, 1,998 third-class; (from 1926) 610 first-class, 950 second-class, 640 tourist-class.
Crew: 972.
Engines: direct acting steam turbines, 62,000shp; quadruple screw, 23kt.
Fate: broken up at Faslane, Gare Loch, February 1950.

Berengaria ex-Imperator (1913-38)
AG Vulkan Werke, Hamburg, launched 23 May 1912.
52,226grt; 909ft loa.
Passengers: (from 1922) 972 first-class, 630 second-class, 606 third-class, 515 tourist-class.
Crew: 1,180.
Engines: direct acting steam turbines, 74,000shp; quadruple screw, 23kt.
Fate: broken up at Jarrow, then Rosyth, November 1938.

Albania (1921-41)
Scotts, Greenock, launched 17 April 1920.
12,768grt; 539ft loa.
Passengers: 480 cabin-class.
Engines: geared steam turbines, 6,800shp; twin screw, 13kt.
Fate: sold for further trading, *California* (1930); torpedoed and sunk, 11 August 1941.

Scythia (1921-58)
Vickers Armstrong, Barrow, launched 22 March 1922.
19,930grt; 624ft loa.
Passengers: (as built) 337 first-class, 331 second-class, 1,538 third-class; (from 1949) 248 first-class, 630 tourist-class.
Crew: 409.
Engines: geared steam turbines, 13,500shp; twin screw, 16kt.
Fate: broken up at Inverkeithing, January 1958.

Samaria (1922-56)
Cammell Laird, Birkenhead, launched 27 November 1920.
19,848grt; 624ft loa.
Passengers: (as built) 350 first-class, 340 second-class, 1,500 third-class; (from 1950) 248 first-class, 641 tourist-class.
Crew: 410.
Engines: geared steam turbines, 13,500shp; twin screw, 16kt.
Fate: broken up at Inverkeithing, January 1956.

Laconia (1922-42)
Swan, Hunter & Wigham Richardson, Newcastle, launched 9 April 1921
19,695grt; 623ft loa.
Passengers: 340 first-class, 340 second-class, 1,500 third-class.
Crew: 410.
Engines: geared steam turbines, 13,500shp; twin screw, 16kt.
Fate: torpedoed and sunk off Freetown by *U156*, 12 September 1942.

Andania (1922-40)
Hawthorn Leslie, Newcastle, launched 1 November 1921.
13,950grt; 538ft loa.
Passengers: 484 cabin-class, 1,222 third-class.
Crew: 270.
Engines: geared steam turbines, 8,500shp; twin screw, 15kt.
Fate: torpedoed and sunk off Iceland by *UA70*, 15 June 1940.

Antonia (1922-48)
Vickers Armstrong, Barrow, launched 11 March 1921.
13,867grt; 540ft loa.
Passengers: 484 cabin-class, 1,222 third-class.
Crew: 271.
Engines: geared steam turbines, 8,500shp; twin screw, 15kt.
Fate: sold to the Admiralty for service as repair ship, March 1942, HMS *Wayland* (1944); broken up, 1948.

Ausonia (1922-65)
Armstrong Whitworth, Newcastle, launched 22 March 1921.
13,912grt; 538ft loa.
Passengers: 510 cabin-class, 1,178 third-class.

Crew: 270.
Engines: geared steam turbines, 8,500shp; twin screw, 15kt.
Fate: sold to the Admiralty for service as repair ship HMS *Ausonia*, June 1942; broken up at Castellon, Spain, August 1965.

Aurania (1924-61)
Swan, Hunter & Wigham Richardson, Newcastle, launched 6 February 1924.
13,984grt; 540ft loa.
Passengers: 500 cabin-class, 1,200 third-class.
Crew: 270.
Engines: geared steam turbines, 8,500shp; twin screw, 15kt.
Fate: sold to the Admiralty for service as repair ship, March 1942, HMS *Artifex* (1944); broken up at La Spezia, January 1961.

Tyrrhenia (1922-40)
William Beardmore, Glasgow, launched 31 May 1920.
16,243grt; 553ft loa.
Passengers: (as built) 265 first-class, 370 second-class, 1,150 third-class; (from 1924) 580 cabin-class, 1,000 third-class.
Crew: 300.
Engines: geared steam turbines, 13,500shp; twin screw, 16kt.
Fate: renamed *Lancastria*, 1924; bombed and sunk off St Nazaire, 17 June 1940.

Franconia (1923-56)
John Brown, Clydebank, launched 21 October 1922.
20,341grt; 623ft loa.
Passengers: (as built) 221 first-class, 356 second-class, 1,266 third-class; (from 1949) 253 first-class, 600 tourist-class.
Crew: 414.
Engines: geared steam turbines, 13,500shp; twin screw, 16kt.
Fate: broken up at Inverkeithing, December 1956.

Carinthia ex-Servia (1925-40)
Vickers Armstrong, Barrow, launched 24 February 1925.
20,277grt; 624ft loa.
Passengers: 240 first-class, 460 second-class, 950 third-class.
Crew: 450.
Engines: geared steam turbines, 13,500shp; twin screw, 16kt.
Fate: torpedoed and sunk off Northern Ireland by *U46*, 6 June 1940.

Alaunia (1925-57)
John Brown, Clydebank, launched 7 February 1925.
14,030grt; 538ft loa.
Passengers: 484 cabin-class, 1,222 third-class.
Crew: 270.
Engines: geared steam turbines, 8,500shp; twin screw, 15kt.
Fate: sold to the Admiralty for service as repair ship, December 1944, HMS *Alaunia* (1945); broken up at Blyth, September 1957.

Ascania (1925-56)
Armstrong Whitworth, Newcastle, launched 20 December 1923.
14,013grt; 538ft loa.
Passengers: (as built) 500 cabin-class, 1,200 third-class; (from 1949) 198 first-class, 498 tourist-class.
Crew: 270.
Engines: geared steam turbines, 8,500shp; twin screw, 15kt.
Fate: broken up at Newport, South Wales, December 1956.

Queen Mary (1936-67)
John Brown, Clydebank, launched 26 September 1934.
81,237grt; 1,019ft loa.
Passengers: (as built) 776 cabin-class, 784 tourist-class, 579 third-class; (from 1947) 711 first-class, 707 cabin-class, 577 tourist-class.
Crew: 1,101.
Engines: geared steam turbines, 212,000shp; quadruple screw, 29kt.
Fate: sold for use as a museum, hotel and convention centre, Long Beach, California, October 1967; still in existence.

Mauretania (1939-65)
Cammell Laird, Birkenhead, launched 28 July 1938.
35,738grt; 772ft loa.
Passengers: (as built) 440 cabin-class, 450 tourist-class, 470 third-class; (from 1947) 475 first-class, 390 cabin-class, 300 tourist-class.
Crew: 780.
Engines: geared steam turbines, 42,000shp; twin screw, 23kt.
Fate: broken up at Inverkeithing, November 1965.

Queen Elizabeth (1940-68)
John Brown, Clydebank, launched 27 September 1938.
83,673grt; 1,031ft loa.
Passengers: 823 first-class, 662 cabin-class, 798 tourist-class.
Crew: 1,296.
Engines: geared steam turbines, 212,000shp; quadruple screw, 29kt.
Fate: sold for use as a museum, hotel and convention centre, Port Everglades, Florida, November 1968, *Elizabeth* (1969); sold for conversion to university ship *Seawise University*, August 1970; destroyed by fire at Hong Kong, 9 January 1972.

Media (1947-89)
John Brown, Clydebank, launched 12 December 1946.
13,345grt; 531ft loa.
Passengers: 250 first-class.
Crew: 184.
Engines: geared steam turbines, 15,000shp; twin screw, 18kt.
Fate: sold for further trading, *Flavia* (October 1961), *Flavian* (1982), *Lavia* (1986); broken up at Kaohsiung, Taiwan, June 1989, after fire at shipyard, 7 January 1989.

Parthia (1948-69)
Harland & Wolff, Belfast, launched 25 February 1947.
13,362grt; 532ft loa.
Passengers: 251 first-class.
Crew: 184.
Engines: geared steam turbines, 15,000shp; twin screw, 18kt.
Fate: sold for further trading, *Remuera* (November 1961), *Aramac* (1964); broken up at Kaohsiung, Taiwan, November 1969.

Caronia (1949-74)
John Brown, Clydebank, launched 30 October 1947.
34,274grt; 715ft loa.
Passengers: 581 first-class, 351 cabin-class.
Crew: 600.
Engines: geared steam turbines, 35,000shp; twin screw, 22kt.
Fate: sold for further trading, *Columbia* (May 1968), *Caribia* (December 1968); wrecked at Apra, Guam while en route to the scrapyard, 12 August 1974.

Saxonia (1954-)
John Brown, Clydebank, launched 17 February 1954.
22,592grt; 608ft loa.
Passengers: (as built) 110 first-class, 819 tourist-class; (from 1963) 117 first-class, 764 tourist-class (one-class when cruising).
Crew: 461.
Engines: geared steam turbines, 24,500shp; twin screw, 20kt.
Fate: renamed *Carmania*, January 1963; sold for further trading, *Leonid Sobinov* (1973); still in service.

Ivernia (1955-)
John Brown, Clydebank, launched 14 December 1954.
22,637grt; 608ft loa.
Passengers: (as built) 110 first-class, 833 tourist-class; (from 1962) 119 first-class, 728 tourist-class (one-class when cruising).
Crew: 461.
Engines: geared steam turbines, 24,500shp; twin screw, 20kt.
Fate: renamed *Franconia*, January 1963; sold for further trading, *Fedor Shalyapin* (1973); still in service.

Carinthia (1956-)
John Brown, Clydebank, launched 14 December 1955.
21,947grt; 608ft loa.
Passengers: 154 first-class, 714 tourist-class (one-class when cruising).
Crew: 461.
Engines: geared steam turbines, 24,500shp; twin screw, 20kt.
Fate: sold for further trading, *Fairland* (January 1968), *Fairsea* (1971), *Fair Princess* (1988); still in service.

Sylvania (1957-)
John Brown, Clydebank, launched 22 November 1956.
22,017grt; 608ft loa.
Passengers: 154 first-class, 724 tourist-class (one-class when cruising).
Crew: 461.
Engines: geared steam turbines, 24,500shp; twin screw, 20kt.
Fate: sold for further trading, *Fairwind* (January 1968), *Sitmar Fairwind* (1988), *Dawn Princess* (1988); still in service.

Queen Elizabeth 2 (1969-)
John Brown, Clydebank, launched 20 September 1967.
66,852grt; 963ft loa.
Passengers: (as built) 564 first-class, 1,441 tourist-class (1,400 single-class when cruising); (from 1972) 604 first-class, 1,223 tourist-class (1,740 single-class when cruising).
Crew: 906.
Engines: (as built) geared steam turbines, 110,000shp; (from 1988) diesel-electric, 130,000bhp; twin screw, 28.5kt.
Fate: still in service.

Olympic (1911-35)
Harland & Wolff, Belfast, launched 20 October 1910.
45,324grt; 882ft loa.
Passengers: 618 first-class, 447 tourist-class, 382 third-class.
Crew: 860.
Engines: triple expansion steam reciprocating plus low pressure steam turbine, 51,000ihp; triple screw, 21kt.
Fate: broken up at Jarrow, then Inverkeithing, October 1935.

Majestic ex-Bismarck (1922-40)
Blohm & Voss, Hamburg, launched 20 June 1914.
56,551grt; 956ft loa.
Passengers: 750 first-class, 545 second-class, 850 third-class.
Crew: 1,000.
Engines: direct acting steam turbines, 86,000shp; quadruple screw, 24kt.
Fate: sold for conversion to Artificer Cadets training ship, July 1936, HMS *Caledonia* (1937); broken up at Inverkeithing, March 1940.

Homeric ex-Columbus (1922-36)
F. Schichau, Danzig (Gdansk), launched 17 December 1913.
34,351grt; 774ft loa.
Passengers: 529 first-class, 487 second-class, 1,750 third-class.
Crew: 730.
Engines: triple expansion steam reciprocating, 32,000ihp; twin screw, 19kt.
Fate: broken up at Inverkeithing, February 1936.

Doric (1923-35)
Harland & Wolff, Belfast, launched 8 August 1922.
16,484grt; 601ft loa.
Passengers: 600 cabin-class, 1,700 third-class.
Crew: 350.
Engines: geared steam turbines, 9,000shp; twin screw, 15kt.
Fate: broken up at Newport, South Wales, October 1935, after collision off the coast of Portugal, 5 September 1935.

Laurentic (1927-40)
Harland & Wolff, Belfast, launched 16 June 1927.
18,724grt; 600ft loa.
Passengers: 594 cabin-class, 406 tourist-class, 500 third-class.
Engines: triple expansion steam reciprocating and low pressure steam turbine, 15,000ihp; triple screw, 16kt.
Fate: torpedoed and sunk off Bloody Foreland, Ireland by *U99*, 3 November 1940.

Britannic (1930-60)
Harland & Wolff, Belfast, launched 6 August 1929.
27,778grt; 712ft loa.
Passengers: (as built) 504 cabin-class, 551 tourist-class, 498 third-class; (from 1947) 429 first-class, 564 tourist-class.
Crew: 500.
Engines: four-stroke double-acting diesels, 17,000bhp; twin screw, 18kt.
Fate: broken up at Inverkeithing, December 1960.

Georgic (1932-56)
Harland & Wolff, Belfast, launched 12 November 1931.
27,759grt; 711ft loa.
Passengers: (as built) 479 cabin-class, 557 tourist-class, 506 third-class; (one class emigrants from 1948).
Crew: 500.
Engines: four-stroke double-acting diesels, 17,000bhp; twin screw, 18kt.
Fate: broken up at Faslane, February 1956.